KU-485-361

A Thought
For Each Day
In 1979

He who sows courtesy reaps friendship,
and he who sows kindness gathers love.

WINTRY DAYS

Sunshine on the frozen snow—
What a cheerful sight!
We long for spring, but winter, too,
Holds many a delight.

DAVID HOPE

JANUARY

<u>MONDAY—JANUARY 1.</u>

JANUARY, as you no doubt know, is named after Janus, the Roman god with two faces — one looking back over the old year, one looking out into the future. I am always reminded of Janus when I visit a certain 17th century walled garden. As you enter through the old gateway you look up and see a smiling face carved into the stone. Once you are in the garden, you see that on the inside of the gateway there is another sculptured face, but this one is scowling at you and putting out its tongue.

I suppose when we look back we can see all kinds of unpleasant things in the year that has passed. But that is all behind us now, and as the church bells peal in the New Year it seems to greet us with a smiling face and promise better things to come.

<u>TUESDAY—JANUARY 2.</u>

SOME thoughts on friendship.

I look upon every day to be lost in which I do not find a new acquaintance.—*Dr Johnson.*

The man who sees a chance to do a good turn here and a little one there, and shed a little light here and a little sunniness there, has something to live for.—*Henry Drummond.*

Of all the joys we can bring into our lives, there is none so joyous as that which comes to us as a result of caring for others and brightening sad lives.—*E. C. Burke.*

To love and be loved is the greatest happiness in existence.—*Sydney Smith.*

The only way to have a friend is to be one.—*Ralph Emerson.*

THE FRIENDSHIP BOOK

A LONDON girl was given a five-year diary as a Christmas present. She hadn't kept a diary before and wondered what on earth to do with it. Then she made up her mind. From New Year's Day she wrote down the things that had given her most pleasure during the day. Little things like a letter from a friend, a game with a playful puppy, the first crocus or daffodil. She called these things " blessings," and sometimes there were several to put down, so that she could scarcely find space for them all. Every day she faithfully made some entry in what she called her " Blessings Book."

When her diary was filled, five years later, she had a book that would cheer her time and time again, for all she had to do was open at any page and recall the countless good moments, the " blessings " she had faithfully recorded in its pages.

JANE had been going through a bad patch. Everything seemed to be getting on top of her. Eventually she suffered a nervous breakdown, and had to spend a week or two in a mental hospital where she was carefully examined and given a course of treatment.

She's back at work now, and coping very well. " I think these new tablets have done me a lot of good," she confided in me the other day. " But not half as much good as my friends at work. Everybody was so helpful and understanding. They pulled me through."

When a sick person is trying to get back on their feet, the doctor's prescription is all very well — but in the end it's the kindness of family and friends that counts.

THE FRIENDSHIP BOOK

MOST of us find it hard to get up on these gloomy winter mornings. When I'm feeling depressed by the sight of a miserable dawn I always cheer myself up with this simple thought: we have passed the Winter Solstice! The longest night is always around the 21st December. After that date the days gradually begin to get longer. It's hardly noticeable at first, but once past the Solstice it is a matter of absolute certainty that the world is getting brighter all the time. So in the darkness of January I just tell myself to be a bit more patient. As the poet remarked: " If Winter comes, can Spring be far behind?"

WHEN she was only four years old Jacqueline Du Pré wanted to play the cello. Two years later she gave her first performance in public, and later became one of the world's most promising young cellists.

Then tragedy struck. When she was only 24 Jacqueline discovered that she had disseminated sclerosis. The real tragedy was that, of all places, it most affected her sensitive fingers, making it impossible for her to continue playing before an audience. But instead of reacting with bitterness she said this: " I have loved the cello and it has brought me so much pleasure. At least I have played the entire repertoire. There is not a single piece written for the cello that I haven't played . . . I have had a very rich, fulfilled life."

GIVE unto the Lord the glory due unto his name.

ROUGH BEAUTY

No grander sight than rugged coast
Where rocks like bastions stand;
The mighty sea may rage and roar —
We're safe upon dry land!

DAVID HOPE

MONDAY—JANUARY 8.

BEN was painting the garden gate as I passed by, his cheery face rosy and shining for it was a cold sharp morning. By his side played a little girl of three or four. " This is Rosie," smiled Ben. " She's come to stay with us for a little while. She's helping me."

The little girl laughed up at me as she dabbed at the gatepost with a small paint brush.

I nodded. Ben and his wife often take in foster children, whose parents are in hospital or unable to care for them for a period. Nothing so unusual about that — except that Ben is confined to a wheelchair and has been since an accident many years ago. He never complains—just the reverse.

" People have been so kind and generous to us," says Ben. " So my wife and I have tried to do our share by looking after these children, although to be honest it has given us so much pleasure that we now do it simply because we like to."

The little girl was still helping Ben when I left — or should I say that they were helping each other.

TUESDAY—JANUARY 9.

I HAVE read scores of definitions of faith. But none for me sums up more beautifully the spirit of the Word than this simple affirmation of faith found scrawled on a cellar wall in Cologne after the holocaust of the last war :

" *I believe in the sun, even when it is not shining. I believe in love, even when I feel it not. I believe in God, even when he is silent.*"

We probably will never know who wrote these words, or in what circumstances. But with faith like that, no one need fear anything the world can do.

THE FRIENDSHIP BOOK

BOB THWAITE, a milkman, told me this story.
It was near the end of the school holidays, and
he was waiting for a customer to fetch her purse.
Her son, a boy of about six, came to the door. Bob
asked if he was looking forward to going back to
school. " No," was the reply.

" But I bet your mum is," Bob smiled. " Oh,
no," answered the boy seriously. " My mum
doesn't go to school. She's been, and she knows
nearly everything."

Well, mums do, don't they?

THE weather forecast's full of gloom,
There's often no denying;
But we can make a local clime
By a little trying,
And with the sunshine of a smile
Send depression flying.

ONE of the best-loved figures of the tennis world
who took part in the parade of former
Champions at Wimbledon's Centenary Celebrations
was the American Doris Hart, Ladies' Singles
Champion of 1951.

But for a childhood misfortune Doris might never
have played the game at all. She was stricken by
polio which left her with a crippled leg and her
parents were advised that she should take up tennis
as exercise for it. So strong was Doris Hart's
determination that she overcame this handicap to
become a world-class player and one who was out-
standingly popular for her sportsmanship.

IN HARBOUR

There's nets to mend and ropes to splice,
  But it's pleasant in the sun,
With time to yarn upon the deck
  While all the work is done.
Then it's out to wind and wave again
  Where livings must be won.

DAVID HOPE

THE FRIENDSHIP BOOK

TAKE time to listen,
  Don't hurry away
When your friends have something
  They want to say.

Take time for a kindness,
  Keep looking about,
There are lots of ways
  You can help someone out.

Give of your friendship
  And you'll find it's true —
The blessings you scatter
  Will come back to you.

TRUST ye in the Lord for ever : for in the Lord Jehovah is everlasting strength.

MY friend Malcolm was telling me he had been shopping with his wife who wanted a dress. They visited umpteen different shops before she found just the one she wanted. Even the price was reasonable.

The salesgirl smiled as she handed over the parcel: " I hope you will enjoy wearing it, madam."

Malcolm's wife was a picture of delight as they left the shop. He told me, " I thought it was because she liked the dress so much, but then she said, ' What a nice thing for the girl to say — " I hope you'll enjoy wearing it !" ' She was really walking on air."

Francis Gay salutes an unknown sales girl!

THE FRIENDSHIP BOOK

WHEN Bing Crosby died of a heart attack in October 1977, millions mourned the loss of one of the world's greatest singers. But many thousands thought of him as a real friend. It is not unusual for stars of stage and screen to be philanthropists, but Bing Crosby's work for charity was quite outstanding.

In 1976, the year before he died, every penny that he earned went to help some worthy cause, quite a lot of it going towards youth work in London. At the age of 73 Bing still had a wonderful voice—but, even more important, he had a warm and generous heart.

WEDNESDAY—JANUARY 17.

MY old Sunday School superintendent was a man with little education, but well able to express himself in simple, direct language. One of the illustrations he used when I was about eleven will remain for ever in my memory. He told us about how, when he was a boy, he had taken part in a competition. The idea was to fill an ordinary matchbox with as many individual objects as possible. He told us what he had crammed into the tiny space available . . . a farthing, a pin, a paper-clip, a grain of rice, various seeds, and so forth. Eventually the boys had to turn out the contents of their match-boxes, and the winner was the one who had collected the greatest number of items.

" Now," he said. " Life is just like that competition. God expects us to fill our lives with as many good and useful things as we can possible cram into them."

A good thing to remember at the start of another year.

THE FRIENDSHIP BOOK

I HEARD recently about a young Glasgow postman. On his round there is an old tenement, and
one day a door on the second floor opened as he went
up the stairs. An elderly lady stood waiting for him.
" Anything for me?" she asked, giving her name. As
he checked his bundle it struck him that he couldn't
recall ever delivering anything there except gas and
electricity bills. As he said, " Sorry, nothing today,"
he sensed the old lady had not really expected anything. Then she said quickly, " Have you a minute to
spare ? I've something I'd like you to see."

Well, bless him, he said he did have a moment to
spare and followed her into her sitting room. What
she had to show him was a TV set. " Isn't it wonderful?" she said excitedly. Then, full of her new
pleasure she asked him if he'd seen a certain pro-
gramme the night before, weren't the nature pro-
grammes wonderful and so on. Quietly the sympa-
thetic young postman agreed, entering into her
obvious pleasure. Then, as he was bidding her a
cheery goodbye, the old woman touched him on the
arm. " Thank you for listening," she said. " I'm so
excited and I had nobody to share it with."

Having no one to share your joys . . . maybe that
is just as bad as having no one to share your worries.

ARTHUR JAMES BALFOUR, once Prime
Minister of Great Britain, declared, " The best
thing to give your enemy is forgiveness; to an
opponent, tolerance; to a friend, your heart; to
a child, a good example; to a father, deference;
to a mother, conduct that will make her proud of
you; to yourself, respect; to all men — charity."

Wise words. Think on them.

SINGING RIVER

So near the busy city throng
The river sings a softer song,
Linger — in time you're sure to hear
A murmur rise, low but clear:
" All that troubles you today
Will, like my waters, pass away."

DAVID HOPE

THE FRIENDSHIP BOOK

WHEN the lamp is lit and darkness
At a touch is put to flight,
Spare a thought for all the folk
Who never know the light,
And make a vow you'll try to shed
Some brightness on the path they tread.

GOD only is my rock and my salvation.

JUD was one of two doctors in an Israeli unit during the Six-Day War of 1967. One of the wounded men who needed his attention paid him this tribute: " I have never met a doctor like Jud. He worked under fire, mocking the bullets, somehow finding the presence of mind to give more than just medical treatment—a comforting smile here, a good word there, a wink, a promise. He worked long hours without stopping, ignoring all danger. A man called Gadi was in bad shape. Jud ordered: ' Talk to him — don't let him fall asleep, or he will never wake up.' In the morning Gadi said ' Am I still here? I thought it was the end — I think I can make it now.'

" ' Of course you'll make it,' declared Jud—and he did. Jud himself wouldn't listen when he was told he was a hero. He kept praising his battalion commander. Said Jud, ' Every word he uttered — even the most casual—inspired calm and confidence.' "

The battalion commander, in his turn, paid tribute to somebody else.

The truth is that real heroes are never aware of being heroes. By their modesty, as well as their bravery, they set us all an example.

THE FRIENDSHIP BOOK

I KNOW a woman who walks a mile every morning to help her mother, who suffers from arthritis, out of bed, and she goes back to make her comfortable at night.

I know another who drives five miles twice a day to cook and dust for an elderly father.

I have heard, too, about Mrs Jean Shaw of Paisley. When Jean was a girl her mother died and she became woman of the house to her father, and mother to her younger sister Ruby. When Jean married, and their father died, she took Ruby to live with her as one of her new family. When Ruby later became ill and had long spells in hospital, Jean popped in to keep her house shining, see Ruby's hubbie had a proper tea at night, and so on.

In towns and villages up and down the country there are women such as these, shouldering responsibilities, keeping a smiling face for their own families and to the world, and getting on with the job. In paying tribute to Mrs Shaw, I salute them all. It's these unsung angels of the duster and the kitchen sink who make the world a better place.

SOME years ago there was a dinner in London for Commonwealth heads of state.

The Chief of Protocol noticed a guest pocket a gold salt shaker. He told Sir Winston Churchill what had happened, and asked what he should do.

" Leave it to me," said Sir Winston, and proceeded to pocket a gold pepper shaker.

He then turned to the guilty party and whispered, " Oh, dear, the Chief of Protocol saw us. We'd better put them both back."

Churchill's diplomacy could save any situation !

THE FRIENDSHIP BOOK

THIS is the time of year when Scots men and women in all parts of the world come together to honour the memory of Robert Burns. He was born on January 25, 1759, in a two-roomed cottage of clay and thatch. A few days after he came into the world, the house was so badly damaged in a gale that young Robert had to be carried into the night to the shelter of a neighbour's house.

The greatest gift of Robert Burns was his ability to put into unforgettable words the simple truths of life. I am thinking as I write of these lines:

> *The heart aye's the part aye*
> *That makes us right or wrang.*

It's so true, isn't it? A good turn done grudgingly, out of a sense of duty, brings true reward neither to the giver nor the receiver. But when the good deed comes from the heart, when service is given with a smile, then a glow comes over life that makes what we have done doubly worthwhile.

THE REV. DICK SHEPPARD, vicar of St. Martins-in-the-Fields, had been to a party one night and on his way home he looked in at his crypt and found a young girl in tears. She had quarrelled with her parents in Leeds, been turned out of the house, and had come to London to earn her living. She had failed and was in despair. Although she didn't actually say so, Dick Sheppard realised that she was homesick.

Without a moment's hesitation, he took the girl to the station and travelled with her on the night train North. First thing in the morning, she was reunited with her parents, whilst Dick Sheppard returned to London, a very weary but happy man.

THE FRIENDSHIP BOOK

YOU haven't heard of David Railton? He was a curate in Folkestone when the First World War ended and he went to see the Dean of Westminster and told him of an idea he had. The Dean of Westminster liked the idea and passed it on it to the Cabinet ministers in Parliament. They accepted the suggestion, and so, on November 11, 1920, as a tribute to the fallen, there was a solemn re-interment in Westminster Abbey.

That spot is the Tomb of the Unknown Warrior, and David Railton's proposal had been that an unidentified soldier should be buried in Westminster Abbey to represent all those who gave their lives during the First World War. Other nations have since copied the idea.

Somehow it seems right and proper that the fame of the Unknown Warrior should be due to an almost unknown curate.

A GOOD name is rather to be chosen than great riches.

THOSE who are permanently confined to bed or a wheelchair with some crippling illness often show a marvellous strength of character. An interesting testimony to such a man can be seen on a tombstone in Avebury Cemetery in Wiltshire:

"*Here lies the remains of S. W. Eilliton. Who during the Boer War suffered an injury causing complete and utter immobility, but somehow ran and caught up, and kept ahead of, the many stresses and strains of this hectic life.*"

THE FRIENDSHIP BOOK

> *SHARE a little, strive a little.*
> *Care a little, thrive a little.*
> *Spend a little, save a little.*
> *Brave a little, bend a little.*
> *Don't belittle, don't be brittle.*
> *Take a little, give a little.*

THIS story came from a night nurse in a Mersey-side hospital.

As she tip-toed among the beds, a frail, elderly woman called her across. " Nurse," she whispered, " would you ask my friend to come?" " Of course," was the reply. " First thing in the morning." The woman clutched her sleeve : " Now, nurse, now. I'll not be here in the morning."

Well, although the nurse and her night sister both believed the old woman was on the mend, they reluctantly contacted the police who went to the friend's door. So, at three o'clock of a wild night lashing with rain, the ward door opened and there stood the patient's friend, a small elderly woman with the rain running off her coat. The nurse took her to her friend's bedside and left them there in the dim light, chatting quietly together.

Towards dawn, she heard a call of " Nurse!" and there was the visitor sitting holding her friend's hand. At first, the patient seemed asleep, but it took only a moment to know that she would see no more tomorrows.

Later, as she saw the friend off, the nurse asked her if she'd been upset when she was called out at that time of night. The old lady replied simply — " Oh, no. She needed me."

A friend indeed.

FEBRUARY

I LIKE to begin the month with a smile.

And there's maybe something more in this story which comes to me from a Glasgow primary teacher.

She'd been explaining fractions to her class of youngsters. Then, to test them, she asked if there was any difference between taking half an orange and taking eight-sixteenths.

They all agreed they were equal, except young Robert. He insisted he'd rather have the half orange. Teacher asked him why.

" Because, miss," he explained, " the more you cut it the more juice you lose."

A young man who'll go far, wouldn't you say?

THERE is a very lovely word,
  Whose letters number six.
It stands for someone who will help
  If you are in a fix.
Someone you can always trust—
  In whom you can confide;
Whose loyalty will never swerve,
  Of whom you speak with pride;
Whose presence is a blessing,
  In times of stress or storm—
Who speaks such words of comfort,
  So loving, and so warm;
Whose every word is genuine,
  Though other folks pretend—
That lovely word of letters six
  Can only be but " Friend."

THE FRIENDSHIP BOOK

CHOOSING a wife — or a husband — is one of life's vital decisions. An aunt of Yehudi Menuhin once gave this advice to the great violinist when he was twenty :

" You need fundamental honesty in a wife more than anything else. By honesty I mean the knowledge that two and two make four and can never be dreamed into making five. Also, the knowledge that real love is not so much admiration as it is the drive to make life easy for the other person."

Not very romantic, perhaps. But I wonder if any marriage has ever succeeded without these conditions.

REJOICE with them that do rejoice, and weep with them that weep.

I WAS visiting a man in hospital who was just getting over a serious operation. I asked him the usual questions about how he was feeling, and whether he was being well looked after. " Oh, I'm fine now," he said, " and the nurses and staff are wonderful—but do you see that man in the bed over there?" I looked across and saw another patient. There was nothing remarkable about him. He seemed just an ordinary chap. " Well," my friend went on, " that man has done me more good than all the treatment and medicine! He has really cheered me up and kept me going."

As the Book of Proverbs said so long ago, " A merry heart doeth good like a medicine."

NEWS BOY

In shine or rain he never fails
To keep us all in touch:
Just a routine paper round—
And yet it means so much.

DAVID HOPE

THE FRIENDSHIP BOOK

VICKI BAUM, whose novel *Grand Hotel* was made into a famous film, had more than her share of ups and downs. She once wrote something about happiness which I have never forgotten. Here it is:

" If there is one thing I really believe it is that in the final summing-up each of us receives the same amount of happiness. I don't mean good luck or success. I mean that clear, sharp singing feeling that is so rare and lasts such a short time. If it would last it wouldn't be happiness any more. If it were our daily bread we wouldn't appreciate it.

" Happiness cannot be forced or coaxed or commanded. It comes all by itself and everyone can be sure to get a share. But this share may be a little bigger if we are ready to be happy; ready and relaxed and willing to recognise the rare bird when it alights in our heart."

FAITH without works is dead. Genuine religious experience and improvement of character go hand-in-hand. I can think of no better illustration of this than the story of a little boy who one day announced to his parents that he had become a Christian.

They were not impressed. For a long time he had been behaving rather badly, and, in particular, he had been teasing the family cat, pulling its tail and annoying it.

" How do you *know* you're a Christian?" asked his parents.

" Well," he replied, " *I* know and God knows." Then, after a pause, he added, " And I think the cat knows."

THE FRIENDSHIP BOOK

I DON'T suppose the name Robert Raikes means anything to you.

It didn't to me, either, till I came across it in a second-hand bookshop. Raikes was the owner of a local newspaper in Gloucester two hundred years ago. He was a kindly man and after visiting the local jail, he printed an article on its deplorable conditions. He was especially horrified at the circumstances of the youngsters there in those days.

From this, Raikes went on to show a strong concern for children generally. He became a strong advocate of Sunday schools as a means of improvement. Perhaps he wasn't the first to think of the idea, but through his newspaper publicity, his energy and his money, the campaign for Sunday schools spread rapidly throughout Britain and was taken up in America too.

No doubt Sunday schools would have come in time, Robert Raikes or no. But they have played such a worthwhile part in so many lives I am especially happy to pass on his name and his story.

OF all the homely things I have,
The nicest is my clock;
It's steady and dependable
And never runs amok!
It has a rhythmic soothing sound,
A soft and gentle tick;
It's such a pleasant friendly noise,
Neither slow nor quick.
Dear old clock — you've kept for years
The same familiar place;
The mantelpiece would be forlorn
Without your shining face.

THE FRIENDSHIP BOOK

A FEW months ago I spent three weeks in hospital. One particular text from the Scriptures kept coming into my mind. It was the phrase used by Jesus in his parable of the sheep and the goats: " When I was sick, ye visited me."

It may not seem much, just calling in to see someone who is ill — but it is a patient's life-line, keeping him or her in touch with the outside world, showing that somebody cares. Remember that whoever you are, you fall into one of two categories. Either you are sick, and you don't need to be reminded how much it helps when you have a visitor. Or you are fit and well — and could cheer somebody up by doing some sick visiting yourself!

SUNDAY—FEBRUARY 11.

FOR God sent not his Son into the world to condemn the world; but that the world through him might be saved.

MONDAY—FEBRUARY 12.

THE American visitor had been able to satisfy his curiosity as to a Scots ancestor, but was just as curious to learn how he had died.

With true Highland courtesy his host did not want to hurt his feelings by disclosing that the man had been hanged for sheep-stealing. So with native tact he explained, " He took part in a public exhibition and the platform collapsed beneath him."

It's so easy to be blunt and hurtful, to use words that can wound deeply. Perhaps the Highlander was carrying things a bit far, but I know one thing— gentle tact never did anyone any harm and has often done a power of good.

BEETHOVEN was a proud man with a keen fighting spirit. Early deafness, therefore, came as a cruel blow. " Poor Beethoven," he wrote to a friend, " there is no outward happiness; you must create it within you . . . "

But he soon found that this intense inner existence had its own rewards: " I must live alone. But well I know that God is nearer to me than to the others of my art; I associate with Him without fear."

A short time later he copied a favourite prayer into a page of his diary:

" In praise of Thy goodness I must confess that Thou didst try with all Thy means to draw me to Thee. Sickness and misfortune didst Thou send upon me to turn my thoughts to my faults. One thing, only, O Father, do I ask: cease not to labour for my betterment. In whatsoever manner it be, let me turn to Thee and become fruitful in good works."

How many of us only begin to know God as a caring friend when our own life-plans have been scuppered!

DO you know the story of the first Valentine? A Roman priest named Valentinus was sentenced to death by the Emperor Claudius II. During the days before his execution, he became friendly with his gaoler's daughter, a blind girl who brought him food.

The night before he died he wrote a letter to her, a note of appreciation, and signed it " From your Valentine." The date was February 14, 270 A.D.

Thus did St Valentine become patron saint of lovers.

THE FRIENDSHIP BOOK

NOT long ago over 200 folk gathered at a farm-house on the island of Islay, off the west coast of Scotland.

They'd come to bid farewell to Leonard Dawson, a young man, only 34, who had come to the island just four years before, fallen in love with it, and bought a farm there. Leonard entered into island life with enthusiasm. In no time he became truly an Islayman. Although he came from Lincolnshire, he felt completely at home among the island's friendly people.

Leonard wished for nothing more than to spend the rest of his life on Islay. But alas, after an illness fought bravely to the end, he passed away. His final wish was to rest on a hilltop on his land.

So after the crowded service in the little Portna-haven church, over 200 silent mourners followed Leonard along the winding road to the foot of Ben Tart a'Mhill. At the farmhouse, the coffin was transferred to an old-fashioned wooden bier. And as the long line of mourners made their way up the steep heathery slopes of the Ben, they stepped forward one by one to help carry their young friend to his last resting-place. By the time they had reached the top, every man had helped to carry Leonard to the hilltop he loved on the island he called home.

PAT is a lady who works as a library assistant. One of her most amusing experiences was when she picked up a book which had just been returned in damaged condition, looking as though it had been badly chewed. She looked at the title. It was: *How to Teach Your Puppy Obedience* . . .

THE FRIENDSHIP BOOK

HERE is the beginning of a letter written to her cousin, Anna, by a girl almost seven years of age. It has no punctuation of any kind, not even capitals: " helen write anna goerge will give helen apple . . ." Not much of a letter, you might think, for a girl of seven. In fact, it was a tremendous achievement, for only three and a half months earlier this girl—totally blind, deaf and dumb from the age of nineteen months—had been taught to communicate by her dedicated teacher.

The letter gives a clue to the girl's name—Helen Keller—but we ought also to remember the name of Annie Sullivan, a teacher of rare patience and insight. No wonder Helen wrote to her two years later, " I cannot know about many things when my dear teacher is not here. I send you five thousand kisses and more love than I can tell."

LET love be without dissimulation. Abhor that which is evil; cleave to that which is good.

YOU'VE got to be careful when speaking to youngsters. What you say, and what they think you're saying, can be quite different!

Like this story, passed on to me from a friend about a little girl who arrived home from her first day at school looking very woebegone.

When her mother asked what was wrong, she explained her teacher had pointed to a desk and told her to " sit for the present."

" I waited all day," she wailed, " but she didn't give me one !"

THE FRIENDSHIP BOOK

D ID you tackle the trouble that came your way
With a resolute heart and cheerful?
Or hide your face from the light of day
With a craven heart, and fearful?
Oh, a trouble's a ton or a trouble's an ounce,
Or a trouble is what you make it,
And it isn't the fact that you're hurt that counts,
But only — how did you take it?

I SUPPOSE you could call this a story of pure deception!

After tea the other evening I met little Morag, a neighbour's daughter, going down the road with a game of snakes and ladders under her arm. She was off, she told me, to see her grandmother who fell on her garden path a few days before and hadn't been out since. Morag explained to me that her granny was bored at being kept indoors, so Morag visits her most evenings, and they often play snakes and ladders or snap. But Granny's eyes aren't as good as they used to be, Morag confided in me, so she sometimes pretends not to see a snap so that Granny gets a chance to win, too.

Well, I hadn't heard about Granny's fall, so I popped in to see her on my way home next day. I mentioned Morag. "Oh, yes," smiled Granny, "she's great fun, and she loves playing snap. Of course," she continued, peering over her specs with her eyes twinkling, "she's still wee, you know, so I sometimes pretend not to see a snap. But truth to tell, I couldn't say which of us enjoys our games more."

There, I told you it was a story of pure deception. But can you wonder I came away smiling?

THE FRIENDSHIP BOOK

WHAT'S the most important lesson a young nurse can learn?

Stewart Macpherson, of Dunfermline, has no doubt. It's T.L.C. He found out the hard way, when he was struck down by a severe heart attack and rushed to Vale of Leven Hospital.

After his own crisis was over, he was able to take notice of what was going on around him. One day, Andrew, the man in the next bed, suddenly started to gasp for breath. Panic filled his eyes, and he had no strength even to reach for his oxygen mask. Quickly a young nurse came and put her arms round the old man's shoulders and swiftly applied the mask. Then she stayed there, her arm round his shoulders while she talked his fear away.

Afterwards, Mr Macpherson couldn't help remarking on the kindly way she'd handled the emergency. The young nurse looked embarrassed. "Just a matter of T.L.C.," she beamed, and went about her duties.

Try as he would, Mr Macpherson couldn't work out what the letters stood for. Eventually he asked the nurse to explain. "Tender Loving Care," was the smiling reply.

It can make all the difference, you know. Out of hospital as well as in it.

I STILL smile when I remember the notice about a forthcoming Sunday evening service which I saw some years ago outside St Peter's Church in the centre of Harrogate. In prominent letters, it announced the details of the time, the preacher and his theme, as follows:

6 p.m.   The Vicar   (The Devil)

THE FRIENDSHIP BOOK

MARION MacLEAN is the Livingston housewife with the magic purse. No matter how it starts the day, each night the purse finishes up stuffed full of notes.

It sounds like a fairy story, but it's absolutely true. You see, every time something nice happens to Marion, as soon as she can afterwards, she writes a note about it and tucks it into her purse. It might simply be a meeting in the street with a friend who's recovering from an illness. Or a compliment from someone at her work, or an endearing sentence from one of her children. If it brightens her day Marion writes a note about it.

The last thing each night, she sits down and reads them. It only takes a minute, yet she seldom fails to be happily surprised at how many lovely moments she has had each day. Like to try it?

BUT Jesus said unto them, It is I; be not afraid.

EVER talk to your pot plants?

Don't worry, lots of people do. And if you're one, you might enjoy this little story passed to me by a neighbour in the garden the other day. Seems he heard his wife encouraging her pot plants when she was watering them one evening. He looked at her, looked at the plants then ventured — " Your talking doesn't seem to be doing much good, dear. They're looking rather peeky."

" Just what I was thinking myself," she replied absently. " I was wondering if they don't understand English. They're African Violets !"

MIRACLE

At evenfall
Give thanks and pray
For the wonder and beauty
Of night and day.

DAVID HOPE

TUESDAY—FEBRUARY 27.

THE little boy arrived home in tears.

When his mother inquired what happened at school he told her that the teacher had asked all those who wanted to go to heaven to put up their hands.

" You put up your hand, I hope?" asked the mother.

" No," he sobbed. " You had told me to come straight home!"

WEDNESDAY—FEBRUARY 28.

THIS is the story of a man remembered by a piece of tapestry. Twenty years ago, Willie Graham was carried into Foresthall Hospital, Glasgow. He suffered dreadfully from rheumatoid arthritis. The only part of his body he could move were his hands, and these only a few painful inches. Willie never complained about the things he couldn't do. He set out to find something he could—he took up tapestry. The nurses threaded needles and, with infinite effort, Willie taught himself to sew the most wonderful pictures — stitch by painful, perfect stitch. Not only that, he wrote letters to friends and other sufferers, hundreds of people all over the world. Few had any idea the time each letter took him.

He became an example of courage, not just to other patients, but to the staff at the whole hospital. For who, with all the blessings of health and movement, could allow themselves to become depressed after seeing Willie at work, meeting life with a smile despite constant pain?

Willie's brave battle is over. Now the last tapestry he worked on is treasured by the staff of G2, the ward where his spirit so nobly reigned and where every stitch was a triumph.

MARCH

THURSDAY—MARCH 1.

SOMETHING like twenty years ago I heard a remark which has stuck in my mind ever since. It was not uttered by a wit or a philosopher, but by an old gentleman who was waiting for a bus. He noticed that a lady next to him in the queue was carrying a bunch of flowers, and he turned and told her how lovely he thought they looked. " Ah," he smiled, " what would we do without flowers?"

What, indeed! We take them so much for granted, but without the beauty of their form, colour and fragrance, life would be unimaginably the poorer. From the most ordinary daisy or dandelion to the most glorious orchid—thank God for flowers!

FRIDAY—MARCH 2.

THERE are few cemeteries in the world which contain more impressive tombs than the Pere Lachaise Cemetery in Paris. Some years ago I spent an hour or so there looking at the elaborate memorials to the great and famous. Then I came to the place where the pianist and composer Frederic Chopin lies buried.

There was just a simple stone slab lying over his grave. On it was carved his name and the dates, 1810-1849, for this brilliant Polish musician had died young.

Then I noticed a tiny bunch of violets which someone had evidently just placed there—possibly a young girl who loved his music . . . I can hardly remember anything now about those expensive memorials, but I shall not forget Chopin's simple grave and the sincerity of that little tribute.

THE FRIENDSHIP BOOK

HILDA HOLMES, of Manchester, sent me this story with a smile.

It's about a little boy who couldn't stop asking questions. All morning, he'd been pestering his mother with " why " this, and " what " that, and " how " the next thing. At length, in sheer exasperation, Mum sighed, " Oh, Hughie, *must* you ask so many questions? Remember, it was curiosity that killed the cat."

For a moment there was silence. Then a small voice said, " Mum — what did the cat want to know?"

HE that cometh to me shall never hunger; and he that believeth on me shall never thirst.

HE'D always had a longing,
  Right from the very start,
To have a little baby son,
  'Twas deep within his heart!
For then he'd have a splendid pal,
  His little boy would grow —
They'd go to football matches,
  They would swim, and fish, and row . . .
But when the nurse came in the room,
  A smile upon her face,
And said to him, " You've got a girl!"
  His heart began to race.
He saw the bundle in her arms,
  He felt a surge of joy,
And looking at his daughter,
  He forgot about the boy!

THE FRIENDSHIP BOOK

TUESDAY—MARCH 6.

JIM LAWSON, of Edinburgh, makes a habit of writing down, in an old desk diary, thoughts or sayings that make him smile and think.

He sent a few to me the other day. And from them I've chosen this one, because I think it may make us all take a new look at ourselves :—

When God measures a man He puts the tape around the heart, not the head.

WEDNESDAY—MARCH 7.

SUZANNE is only five — but she's learning fast ! The other day, her Grandpa lent her his loose change so she could play at shops with her friend. There was about 30p or so, all in coppers. And as Grandpa rose to leave, he told Suzanne she could keep it.

"What ?" she said, eyes wide. "Oh, no, that's far too much — it would never go in my little purse." Then, with a smile of beguiling innocence, she put her hand in Grandpa's and looked up at him.

"I'll tell you what," she said. "Just give me a 50p piece instead . . !"

THURSDAY—MARCH 8.

IT'S all too easy for Christian preachers and speakers to seek credit for themselves rather than glory for God, and to hope for a word of praise about the quality of the sermon or address. So I like the simple little admonition which I once saw written on the inside of a pulpit, where a visiting preacher could not miss it. Taken from St John's Gospel, it was completely out of context— but forcibly reminded the preacher what he was there for : " Sir, we would see Jesus !"

FRIDAY—MARCH 9.

NANSEN, the famous explorer, told the legend of a monk who had wandered into the fields, above which a lark was singing. The monk had never heard a lark before, and he stood there entranced until the bird and its song had become part of the heavens. When he went back to the monastery he was met by a strange doorkeeper. Other monks appeared, and they were all strangers to him. He told them he was Father Anselm, but that was no help. Finally they looked through the books of the monastery. They revealed that there had been a Father Anselm there a hundred or more years before.

Time had been blotted out while he stood listening to the lark.

It's a beautiful legend! Think of it next time you hear a lark sing.

SATURDAY—MARCH 10.

WHAT happens to you isn't really so important as how you take it.

When something hits you so hard it threatens to sink you, you can either lie down and go under, or stand up, do your level best to keep your head above water, and make the best of it with a smile. That's the hard thing to do, but it's always the best way in the end.

I'm reminded of the words of the great American humorist, Josh Billings. He put it in a nutshell. Said Josh, " The best medicine I know for rheumatism is thanking the Lord it ain't gout !"

SUNDAY—MARCH 11.

BE not overcome of evil, but overcome evil with good.

THE FRIENDSHIP BOOK

A WISH of yours has come to naught,
Some dream has not come true,
The hopes you cherished — one by one,
Alas, they've died in you.
Yet in your heart, if one small flame
Still flickers, then you may
Somehow, some time, dream other dreams
That will come true some day.

I ONCE had the privilege of meeting Lord Inman, a peer of the realm who has been Chairman of the BBC, Lord Privy Seal, and for more than half a century the driving force behind the famous Charing Cross Hospital. Now he is in his eighties, and he loves to talk of his childhood in the picturesque old town of Knaresborough in North Yorkshire.

He started life in the most humble circumstances, living with his brothers and his widowed mother in a thatched, white-washed cottage. He told me how he used to hold the lantern for his mother in the nearby churchyard as she went after nightfall to earn a little extra money by scrubbing the gravestones clean. They were so poor that his mother regularly bought a sheep's head for threepence. " The first day," he said, " we had the broth, the second day the tongue and the brains and the third day the rest of the head."

Such was the meagre fare of a man who has since dined at sumptuous tables with the highest in the land. Now he often looks back to those early days of hardship, and in his mind's eye he sees a vivid picture of his mother, whose love and self-sacrifice he will treasure for the rest of his days.

THE FRIENDSHIP BOOK

IT'S great fun being a member of a dramatic society, even if the plays you act in are not world-shattering. You learn something about yourself, too.

I was walking home with young Alan from our casting meeting. We had been choosing who would play what in our next production. Peter, who is a very bright young man, had been given the leading role.

As we ambled along he began reading the author's description of the part he would have to play. It went like this :

" John Rollins is an up-and-coming young businessman. He does not stand fools easily. He is witty and tends to ride roughshod over the opinions of others——"

Peter stopped suddenly.

" Gosh !" he said. " I hope they didn't choose me for the part because they think I'm like that !"

I quickly assured him that nobody thought he was the least like that unpleasant young man. But his remark left me thinking hard. In a real-life role, how do you and I appear to those watching us? Reliable or dodgy? Selfish or considerate? Mean or generous?

We're sometimes far from being the characters we like to think we are.

MAGISTRATE, addressing a schoolmaster who had been summoned for speeding, " For thirty years I have been waiting for a schoolmaster. Now sit down at that bench and write out five hundred times, ' I must not speed.' "

A taste of his own medicine !

REAPING THE SEA

The labours of the day are done,
Another harvest safely won.
And so it goes, tale without end,
The sea, now enemy, now friend:
So fishermen take smooth with rough
And for each day each day's enough.

DAVID HOPE

THE FRIENDSHIP BOOK

A PHYSICS student at Magdalene College, Cambridge, was asked in an examination, " Describe a common pump."

Now he knew what a pump looked like, but he hadn't the faintest idea how it worked. However, he could draw a bit. So on his examination paper there gradually took shape a picture of a typical village green, featuring an old church porch, the parish beadle in all his pomp and splendour, and the women of the village milling around the village pump, each one with some sort of utensil for carrying water. Nobody was getting any, though, for the pump was chained and padlocked and hung on it was a notice, " This pump locked during Divine Service."

The student was the future writer and poet Charles Kingsley. I don't know what kind of mark he was awarded for his drawing, but I think he deserved one or two at least for ingenuity !

THE Rev. Arthur G. Hopkins is still remembered as a good man. When there was a coal strike a number of years ago, a friend of his met him carrying a bucket of coal along the street late at night. He was unmercifully chaffed for stealing coal during the shortage.

It was not discovered until much later that he had been taking it from his own cellar to give to an old friend who was in great need.

RECOMPENSE to no man evil for evil. Provide things honest in the sight of all men.

THE FRIENDSHIP BOOK

I WAS browsing through a most interesting book in the Episcopal Cathedral of St Mary's in Edinburgh. At first I thought it was the usual visitors' book, then I realised that it was a record of requests for intercessory prayer. As I turned over the pages, I was struck by the great variety of things prayed for. There were folk with all kinds of personal problems, those with loved ones awaiting an operation, students about to take an important exam, even children who wanted a prayer said for some pet animal.

But the most unusual request of all was this, short and to the point :

"*I need a husband. Please pray for me.*"

There was no signature, but whoever this good lady was, I left the church sincerely hoping that in her loneliness she would find a suitable marriage partner and that with him she would live happily ever after.

THE name of Henry Ford is well known as the American founder of the Ford Motor Company, but there is one incident in his life that is seldom remembered today. At the time of the First World War he was horrified at the terrible carnage that was taking place in Europe. As a very wealthy and powerful man, he decided to do something about it. In 1915 he sailed for Europe declaring he would speak to world leaders and hoped to have all the armed forces back in their homes by Christmas.

Alas, it was a forlorn hope. He returned home disillusioned. But although he failed, one can't help admiring the courage of Henry Ford, the man who tried to stop a war single-handed.

THE FRIENDSHIP BOOK

A MESSAGE in a bottle isn't too uncommon, but I found one in a cork, on, of all places, the desk of a friend. He has a spike on to which go small pieces of paper he hasn't quite finished with. The point is sharp so my friend keeps a champagne cork on it. When I suggested he should get a new one, he explained that in 1942, when he was in the R.A.F., he suddenly got seven days' embarkation leave before being sent to North Africa. Like thousands of others in those days, he didn't know what lay ahead. But he and his fiancee decided that rather than wait, they'd get married on that leave. Somehow they managed to get hold of a bottle of champagne on their short honeymoon.

One day soon after he was demobbed in 1945, he said to his wife, " Now we'll start to get some bits and pieces of our own together." She laughed, and, saying she'd already started, drew from her handbag the champagne cork. She explained she'd kept the cork through all the days he'd been abroad, as a memento of their short happiness together and a hope for the future.

Sentimental? I daresay, but my friend set the cork in front of him in the office. It's been there ever since, a symbol of his wife's hope and faith during their separation, and a challenge and a beacon for his marriage over the years since.

THURSDAY—MARCH 22.

ALEX. COMFORT, the writer, advised folk who felt " past it " to remember the man of 104 who, when he complained of a painful stiff right knee was told, " After all, you can't expect to be agile at your age." He immediately retorted, " My left knee is 104, too, and *that* doesn't hurt!"

FRIDAY—MARCH 23.

IN front of me as I write are four photographs of Victor Hugo, the great French poet and novelist. They were taken about 1880 when he was an old man, very depressed as a result of recent disappointments and bereavements. The first three photographs show him looking desperately sad and forlorn. The photographer had done everything possible to get him to smile, but completely failed.

Then he had an idea. He suddenly brought Hugo's three-year-old grand-daughter into the room. The old man's face lit up with a radiant smile — and the fourth photograph captured it . . .

Is there anything in the whole world which fills us with such hope and cheer as the sight of a little child?

SATURDAY—MARCH 24.

WHAT is a mother?

I think you will find much of the answer in these simple lines from Mrs Haig, of Winchburgh :

She always leaned to watch for us, anxious if we were late, in winter by the window, in summer at the gate; and though we mocked her tenderly, who took such foolish care, the long road home would seem more safe because she waited there.

Her thoughts were all so full of us, she never could forget, and so I think that where she is, she must be waiting yet; waiting till we come home to her, anxious if we are late, watching from Heaven's window, leaning o'er Heaven's gate . . .

SUNDAY—MARCH 25.

FOR where your treasure is, there will your heart be also.

THE FRIENDSHIP BOOK

RACHEL is a nurse in an orthopaedic ward, ministering all day to people with broken bones. Like all nurses, she is kept very busy, and so are the surgeons. "But, you know," she remarked to me the other day, "we do very little, really. We just help the body to heal itself."

How true this is, especially when we think of the way fractured bones knit together. No machine is capable of repairing itself, yet when a bone is broken special cells are automatically released which produce calcium salts, gradually forming a gristly callous which holds the broken ends together. In a matter of weeks the callous hardens into real bone, forming a rather clumsy bulge. Cells of a different type are now released, which miraculously eat away the excess bone. They do their work so well that sometimes a later X-ray cannot detect where the fracture occurred—as in the case of Rachel's sister Ann, whose thigh was shattered by a pony kick when she was only three, and whose leg is now perfectly normal.

Just another illustration of the point made by the great French pioneer of surgery, Ambroise Pare, when he said of a patient more than 400 years ago, " I dressed his wounds. God healed him."

A song, a smile, a kiss—these are the things,
Greater than all the riches of mighty kings.

THESE simple lines by the late Joe Corrie, the Scottish miner poet, remind us that wealth is as nothing compared with the ordinary, homely things in life and the friendship and love of family and friends.

WEDNESDAY—MARCH 28.

HAVE you heard the parable of the donkey? It was sent to me by Gerard McDonald of Glasgow. A father and son set out to market, the father riding the donkey and the son walking alongside.

A passerby jeered at the father for riding while his son walked. Ashamed, the man changed places. Then a woman called out, " A fine son, to let his father walk and ride himself." So they both walked till another passerby called them daft for walking while a big donkey could carry them both, whereupon they both got on the donkey.

A little farther on, they were told they ought to be ashamed of themselves, two people on a poor donkey. Confused that everything they did seemed wrong, they got a pole, tied the donkey's legs together, hung it on the pole and carried him. When they got to the market, everyone burst out laughing. " Look at these silly fools," they cried, " carrying a donkey instead of letting it carry them."

The father and son put the donkey down and the father exclaimed, " By trying to please everyone, son, we've pleased no one. In future, we will do what we believe to be right no matter what anybody says."

Change direction with every wind that blows, and you'll never steer a course of your own.

THURSDAY—MARCH 29.

MY doctor is a marvellous man — efficient, thorough, never in a hurry, always ready to listen. But there are also three even better doctors any of us can consult at any time. " The three best doctors in the world," wrote Dean Swift, " are Dr Diet, Dr Quiet and Dr Merryman."

THE FRIENDSHIP BOOK

FRIDAY—MARCH 30.

THE lovely Parish Church of Knaresborough in Yorkshire has stood there since at least Norman times, and its ancient stonework provides fascinating study. But for sheer human interest there is nothing like the old gravestones which surround it. Some tell tragic tales of young death, but here is a cheerful example, with a quaint bit of spelling :

Sacred to the memory of the agreeable and good
MRS DOVE
Whose life was one continued practice of every Christian virtue Insomuch that any attempt of describing her perfections Would really be an inguery to her character.
Died 1759 — *Aged* 99.

It must have been good to know Mrs Dove.

SATURDAY—MARCH 31.

IF you are not a car owner, there's no boon like a bus — provided there is one when you want it, and it's not too crowded. Have you ever wondered who first got the idea of introducing an " omnibus " — the Latin word meaning "for all"? It was a French thinker called Blaise Pascal who lived in the 17th century. He was a child prodigy in mathematics and a brilliant scientist, but he gave up his career in order to write in defence of Christianity. Though he was acclaimed as a genius and even called the greatest Frenchman of all, he was a very humble man always helping the poor and under-privileged.

One day he asked himself: " Why should only rich people be able to ride in carriages?" His answer was to provide a coach service which could be used by ordinary people on payment of a small fare. It ran across Paris in 1662 — the first bus service in the world.

HER HERO

A guardsman's turn-out is so terribly smart,
From the plume on his helmet right down to his feet,
No wonder a lady can quite lose her heart —
When he kneels down before her, her bliss is complete.

DAVID HOPE

APRIL

ONE of his disciples said unto him, Lord, teach us to pray.

THE following letter came to me from Carlisle:
"Dear Francis Gay — All of us here in the Aglionby Grange Rest Home, Carlisle, are in our 80's and 90's. Some of us are far from well. We all need attention. Sometimes some of us are grumpy. But Mrs Winnie McNaughton never fails to make us comfortable and always with a smile. She works long hours but is always bright and cheerful. You've no idea what a tonic it is just to see her come into the room.

"Recently she went straight off duty to journey to her home town, Perth. She came straight back to duty with as cheery a face for us as ever. Only later did we find out that her short break was to see her ill sister and be present at her passing. It is typical of Winnie that she left her own troubles outside and was as bright as ever with us.

"So often good people are paid their tributes when they're no longer here to know what others think of them. Winnie retires soon, and all here would like her to realise, now, that when she leaves we will feel that the sun has gone out of our lives. We cannot give her much, but she has our love.—Stanley Jackson, for all at The Grange."

I am proud, indeed, to add my own tribute to Winnie, and all like her who bring sunshine into the lives of those who deserve it most.

THE FRIENDSHIP BOOK

TUESDAY—APRIL 3.

ON one occasion in Canada, Olave Baden-Powell, World Chief Guide, was staying with a guide president who told her that her daughter would be among the guides at a big rally that afternoon. The Chief Guide at once said: "When I am inspecting her company, do ask her to tell me who she is."

Later, as she was walking down the lines of Guides at the rally, she was immensely amused to hear a small voice pipe out: " I'm my mother's daughter !"

WEDNESDAY—APRIL 4.

MOST of you will have heard of Helen Keller. Born blind and deaf, and growing up wild, undisciplined and unable to talk, she was taken in hand by a firm, understanding and devoted teacher from whom she learned not only to speak but that life could still be rich and full. So much so that when she died, Helen Keller was honoured everywhere.

I was reminded of her when I called not long ago on my friend Nancy, who is blind and bedridden. She raised a hand towards the window where stood a splendid bunch of daffodils. " They're beautiful, aren't they?" she smiled. " Yes," I said, "but how do you know, without seeing them?"

Nancy smiled again, and told me that once Helen Keller was asked if she could think of any affliction or handicap worse than blindness. For a moment Helen had paused. Then she nodded. " Yes," she said, " to have eyesight and not be able to see."

It was Nancy's way of telling me that, though blind, she has another kind of vision which many with perfect eyesight can never share and which turns her world of darkness into one of light and beauty.

THURSDAY—APRIL 5.

FRANCIS DUCKWORTH likened life to a song. Our experiences, he said, are like notes arranged on a staff. If they are arranged in disorder they cause discord, so they must be set to the principles of harmony to make sweet music that will spread around the world.

Francis worked in his uncle's grocery shop at Stopper Lane, near Rimmington, Yorkshire, and more than once joined in discussions with customers about the merits of hymn-writers. His Uncle John often recited a line from a Watts hymn, " Jesus shall reign where'er the sun !" " He says more in one line than a lot of them say in a whole hymn," said Uncle John, and Francis never forgot the glorious look on his face.

Thirty years later, Francis composed a tune for " Jesus shall reign where'er the sun "— he called it " Rimmington " and it went around the world, and was even included in an African hymnal. The tune was inscribed on his tombstone in the churchyard at Gisburn—the notes and experiences of a lifetime, arranged in order and harmony.

FRIDAY—APRIL 6.

DADDY was tired when he got home from work. " Play with us," pleaded eight-year-old Jimmy and his slightly younger sister Betty from their perch in the oak tree.

" After tea," said Daddy.

" Pleeeease, Daddy," persisted Betty.

" After tea," said Daddy in his cross voice, settling into a deckchair.

" Jimmy," he called, " fetch me the paper and my pipe—there's a good boy !"

" After tea, Daddy," said Jimmy, equally firmly.

SATURDAY—APRIL 7.

AT one of the first meetings of the newly-elected Senate of the United States, a boy called Johnny Jones was present, accompanied by his father. From his place in the gallery, Johnny observed an elderly man rise before the opening of the session. Pointing him out to Johnny, his father explained that he was the Chaplain.

" Oh," said the boy. " He prays for the Senate, doesn't he?"

" Well, no," replied his father, " not exactly. He gets up, has a good look at the Senate, and after that he turns round and prays for the country !"

SUNDAY—APRIL 8.

FOR the Son of man is come to seek and to save that which was lost.

MONDAY—APRIL 9.

IT was spring-time and we were very busy one evening with various jobs round the house — all part of the inevitable spring-cleaning. At the most awkward moment the door-bell rang. " Oh, I'll go and see who it is," said my wife rather wearily. She came back with a smile on her face, holding a tiny posy of flowers. " It was two little girls," she said. " You know, the two from number twelve. They just said, ' Would you like these?' and handed me the flowers. They had a few more little bunches, and they seem to be going round giving them to all the neighbours. They didn't want any money !"

Wasn't that nice ? We hear so much about money-grabbing materialism, but there were two little girls going round giving away little posies of flowers, just because it seemed a good thing to do.

THE FRIENDSHIP BOOK

STANLEY BALDWIN was a very unhappy man towards the close of his life. His wife had died, and a lot of people seemed to be blaming him for the outbreak of the Second World War.

And then one of his friends on a rare visit to London met him and noticed that Baldwin looked far more cheerful than he had done for a long time.

It turned out that Winston Churchill had invited Baldwin for lunch, and afterwards had confided in him some of the most secret questions of the war, and asked him for his opinion.

Maybe Winston Churchill did not really need Lord Baldwin's opinion, but with his intuitive sympathy he knew it would please an old and ailing man who could be trusted not to divulge anything that he had been told.

THE writer, Henry Van Dyke, 1852-1933, revealed the secret of his own strength when he wrote the following lines :

With eager heart and will on fire
I sought to win my great desire;
Peace shall be mine, I said, but life
Grew more bitter in endless strife.

My soul was weary and my pride
Was wounded deep; to heaven I cried
God give me peace or I must die.
The dumb stars glittered no reply.

Broken at last I bowed my head,
Forgetting all myself and said:
Whatever comes, God's will be done,
And in that moment peace was won.

TREASURE TROVE

We search for them as treasures now
  And show them off with pride:
Odds and ends of bygone days
  Which once we threw aside!

DAVID HOPE

THE FRIENDSHIP BOOK

ROBERT HYDE, pastor of Salendine Nook Baptist Church at Huddersfield in the mid-nineteenth century, paid this tribute to his doctor after his death :

" A more generous man never lived. He would drop in when he was passing even if we did not summon him. He would never take a penny piece from me for his services. He was exceedingly good to the poor. It was common talk that he would take more trouble over a sick person from whom he could not hope to receive a penny than over a man who lived in a mansion. He said they needed it more. And they say that some little time before he died he burnt all his account books, for, said he, ' The rich won't pay, the poor can't pay, so what is the use of books anyway?' "

—And we are not even told the good doctor's name !

IT'S great to be good at something but better still to be better — if you see what I mean. You might think that when a man has represented his country at a sport many times he would feel that he knew all there was to be known.

Not so with Basil D'Oliviera, that most popular of cricketers. Even now, near the end of a long and successful career, he still reads every book on the game he can lay hands on. Not long ago he told an interviewer, " I'm always learning something new."

Isn't that the recipe for a full life? However old we are, we can always be on the look-out for new and surprising things. If we keep learning we will never be bored.

SATURDAY—APRIL 14.

A FEW wise words on the subject of friends and friendship.

"THE only way to have a friend is to be one." (R. W. Emerson).

" Let us keep our friendships in repair. They are worth while spending time on and keeping them up, because they constitute a large part of our lives." (Henry Drummond).

" A friend should bear his friend's infirmities." (Shakespeare).

" Give thy love freely, do not count the cost: So beautiful a thing was never lost." (Ella Wheeler Wilcox).

SUNDAY—APRIL 15.

I AM the good shepherd: the good shepherd giveth his life for the sheep.

MONDAY—APRIL 16.

AWAY in the Shropshire hills lived an old man who was not ashamed to talk to God. He kept a chair at his bedside for God, and every night he talked to him there.

When the local vicar called one day and noticed the chair drawn up, he commented to the old man, " So you have had a visitor?"

" Yes," he replied, in his old-fashioned way, " I am never alone. God is wonderfully good. When I come home in the evening I just sit down and think about Him and He comes right into my life."

And when he died a few years later, no one was surprised that his eyes were turned towards his Friend in the chair.

THE FRIENDSHIP BOOK

TWELVE-YEAR-OLD Timothy went running home the other day, beaming all over his face. " Dad!" he shouted. " Guess what!" And he told his father how he had been playing cricket with three other boys on the edge of the local cricket field. A man who was busy sorting out equipment in the nearby pavilion called across to the boys and asked for a volunteer. Thinking some hard work was involved, three of the boys ignored him and went on playing—but Timothy went to offer his services.

" So you're the only volunteer, are you?" said the man. " Well, that makes my job easier. I was trying to decide which one of you lads to give this to. Here you are—it would be a shame to throw it away."

And he handed over a handsome cricket bat, somewhat battered, but far better than the one Timothy had. I shall long remember this man's original combination of generosity and justice, and the look of delight on Timothy's face. You'll never persuade *him* to follow the cynical rule " Never volunteer for anything."

IT'S surprising how many folk have a secret fear they don't like anybody to know about.

Lord Roberts was a courageous Field Marshal, but he was so afraid of cats that he could not enter or stay in a room if he knew one was there.

I have friends who can't bring themselves to step into a lift. Others won't fly in an aeroplane, and one woman is terrified of birds.

You don't have any fears like these? Then thank your lucky stars — and be ready to offer understanding and a helping hand to those who do.

THE FRIENDSHIP BOOK

TWO monks decided that, to enliven the monotony of their existence, they would have a quarrel.

"But what shall we quarrel about?" said one of them.

"We will take this stone and put it between us and I will say, 'This stone is mine.' Then you must reply, 'No, it is mine,' and so we will quarrel."

So they began. "This stone is mine," said the first monk.

"I think the stone is mine," the other gently responded.

"If the stone is thine, then take it," answered the one, and the dispute ended on the spot.

The fact was, they were both so peace-loving in spirit that they simply could *not* quarrel.

WALKING across a golf course on holiday I met an old gentleman giving a lesson to a youngster of ten or eleven, who, I supposed, was his grandson.

The youngster had hit a good shot but the ball had landed up in a weedy hollow, leaving him a very bad lie.

"That's not fair," the youngster complained. "I hit a good shot and it oughtn't to have finished up like that."

"Maybe it shouldn't," said his grandfather, "but it did!" He went on. "It's just the rub of the green. And if you're not going to accept it you should find some other game."

That's life, isn't it? We have to try to overcome our bits of bad luck. Keep complaining and we'll be miserable. Try to rise above them and we often surprise ourselves how well we do.

SPRING SONG

Blossom and bud, with winter gone,
Joyfully have their fling,
And daffodils dancing on the lawn
Trumpet the news of spring.

DAVID HOPE

SATURDAY—APRIL 21.

IF you're sometimes too busy to listen to the children, take warning.

Little Albert's mum was up to the eyes one washday when he asked if she'd play with him.

" Oh, I'm in the middle of the washing, Albert," she replied. " Can't you go and play something by yourself?"

Half an hour later Albert came into the kitchen again. " I've been playing postman," he told her proudly. " I've posted a letter in every door in the street."

" Where on earth did you get them?" asked Mum.

" In your dressing table," he replied, " all tied up in pink ribbon!"

SUNDAY—APRIL 22.

FOR the earth is the Lord's, and the fulness thereof.

MONDAY—APRIL 23.

THE father of famous writer Ursula Bloom was staying at Warwick Castle whilst helping Lady Warwick to write a book. He did all the research. Five-year-old Ursula went with him one week and was playing in the garden with Lady Warwick's son " when a bearded old gentleman came to us and gave us half a crown. I had never seen so much money before ! He said, ' You two slip out and get yourselves some sweets, and don't come home until you have eaten the lot, because if you do they will only take them away from you !' "

Although Ursula Bloom never forgot how sick she felt afterwards, she still delights in recalling the only time she ever met King Edward VII.

THE FRIENDSHIP BOOK

I'VE sat on cosy sofas, on couches filled with hairs,
*   On wickerwork and basket, on cane and easy-*
*   chairs ;*
On rockers, and on pullmans, with cushions in galore,
I've sat on priceless heirlooms that people keep in store.
But the one that was so restful, so comfy and so good,
Wasn't made of leather, or even carved from wood,
Not Chippendale or Sheraton, or any kind of hide —
But nature's lovely grassy bank out in the countryside!

FOR twenty-three years, John Lester was the much-loved chaplain to the residents of Belmont Eventide Home, at Meigle, in Perthshire. His work was done entirely without financial reward, in addition to the ministry of his parish of Lundie and Muirhead.

His sudden death brought great sadness to the men and women of Belmont. Year after year he took a Sunday service at the Home. Old folk do not always hear too well, but they never had any difficulty in hearing " Paddy " Lester as his friends affectionately called him.

But plenty of ministers have a loud voice. Not all have that other quality that John Lester brought to Belmont. One day one of his parishioners asked him, " What do you say in your sermons to the old folk?"

John Lester replied simply: " Exactly the same message as I give in my own church. If it's right there, it's right everywhere."

The point is this. Some people, ministers included, think that because men and women have become old, and perhaps slower than they used to be, they should talk down to them. This can be very hurtful. And, it's a mistake Paddy Lester never made.

THE FRIENDSHIP BOOK

HAIL the dancing daffodils,
*   The very breath of spring!*
They come to keep you company,
*   Both joy and hope they bring.*
How dare you still be miserable,
*   Note well their golden cheer,*
You know they herald sunny days
*   To brighten up your year!*

MRS MARGARET HAYES, of Kirkcaldy, lost her husband after a long and weary illness borne with patience and courage.

As all who've lost a loved one know, so many little things can bring back the pain of such a loss — yes, even the TV licence. When it came up for renewal, Mrs Hayes had to write away for it herself, explaining to the main National TV Licence Records Office that her husband had died. Then she posted her letter, and that seemed to be that.

But a little later, back came her new TV licence. Without thinking much about it, Mrs Hayes opened the envelope and took out the form to put it safely away. That's when she noticed there was something else there — and when she looked again, she found a wee message of sympathy, just a few words hoping that peace, comfort and blessing might be hers. No name — nothing else. Just a quiet and sincere message from someone unknown who had paused for a moment to think of her.

" Imagine," she said, " some person in that soulless set-up bothering to go to that trouble! Humanity can be so marvellous at times, it gives you hope for the world yet."

Indeed it does, Mrs Hayes.

HARMONY

Lift up your hearts! There's beauty here
To cheer the fainting soul;
Nature's perfect harmony
Shall make our spirits whole.

DAVID HOPE

THE FRIENDSHIP BOOK

SATURDAY—APRIL 28.

H E'S a merry little urchin, with a head of tousled
hair,
His hands are very grimy and his knees are red and
bare;
But he answers me politely and remembers to say
" Pardon?"
And always is so careful when he comes inside my
garden!
I really should be angry and make him stay away,
For his ball is lying on my path a dozen times a day;
But Billy has an asset, my heart he'll always win —
When he crinkles up his merry eyes and gives his
cheeky grin!

SUNDAY—APRIL 29.

E VERY one which seeth the Son, and believeth
on him, may have everlasting life.

MONDAY—APRIL 30.

L OUISE DE BOURBON-CONDE, a member
of one of the royal families of France, became
destitute when her family had to flee during the
time of Revolution. She became a nun, and in due
course a much loved Abbess.

Once she heard that a poor man had been for-
bidden to enter the church because his clothes were
verminous and in rags. She made him a whole new
outfit of clothing so that he could go into the church
without shame or embarrassment.

Later, she learned that his new clothes had been
stolen from him by a gang of thieves. Louise at
once set to and made him a new lot.

Such was the generosity of a French princess
who had herself known what it was to be destitute.

MAY

DR PERCY STOCK, whose brother was pastor of Salendine Nook Baptist Church, Huddersfield, was once left at home on Sunday morning to look after two little nieces. After a time one of the girls asked if they might play at having Chapel.

Their uncle remarked that this would be quite proper, but of course she would have to preach a sermon. To this she agreed. She used the back of an armchair as a pulpit while the " congregation " sat on a stool in front. Then she leaned over her "pulpit" and solemnly said, " You must be good. Amen."

It was the shortest — and one of the best — sermons Dr Stock ever heard!

A LIBRARIAN friend told me this story. He got to know an old lady who was a regular user of the library, but always returned her books a few days late. She would smilingly pay the fines on each occasion, but my friend could tell she hadn't a lot of money to spare so one day he asked her if she had difficulty in coming to the library. " Oh, no, dear," she said sweetly, " but you're all so friendly and helpful I always keep my books overdue so that I can make a little contribution."

My friend was touched by her kind thought, but he pointed out gently that really she could show her appreciation best by returning her books on time. So now the library has fewer overdue books to deal with — and one old lady has a few more pennies in her purse!

THE FRIENDSHIP BOOK

I MUST say I like these ten-second sermons that come my way, and here's the latest collection —

Don't give up when the clouds surround you. It can be a sign you're climbing higher.

It's wise to pick your friends — but not to pieces.

Religion was meant to be our steering wheel — not our spare wheel.

When you come to the end of your tether, remember that God is at the other end.

A lie can travel the earth while truth is still getting its shoes on.

Swallowing your pride will never give you indigestion.

Success is to do more for the world than the world does for you.

BOB HENDERSON, of Restalrig, Edinburgh, tells me of an old lady who went to Waverley Station recently to ask about reserving a seat to Aberdeen.

The clerk helped her to choose the best train, wrote down times of departure and arrival for her, and assured her that, even though there was a dining-car, nobody would mind in the slightest if she took her own tea and sandwiches.

Then, just as she was about to go, she remembered something else. " If there was to be a crash," she said, " which would be the most dangerous coach to be in?"

The clerk could only guess. " The last one, I think," he replied.

" Well," said the old soul, shaking her head, " it's a wonder they don't take it off."

WELCOME

Spring is come — the patient buds
Now burst to greet the sun,
And cottage gardens all rejoice:
The winter's past and done!

DAVID HOPE

THE FRIENDSHIP BOOK

YOU could say that John Kyle of Springburn, Glasgow, read gas meters. And it would be true.

But he did much more. He helped to shape the lives of a thousand boys. For more than 35 years John was captain of the 200th Boys' Brigade Company. Many of his lads came from poor homes. Many had been in trouble. But always he looked for the gold he believed lay in every boy, and almost always he found it.

Indeed, I am told one of them once landed in Borstal, not long before the annual summer camp. John went to the governor, and asked to be allowed to take the boy with him to camp. Well, it was a risk, but the governor finally agreed. John knew all that the lad needed was to believe somebody trusted him. It proved to be the turning point in the boy's life. He never put a foot wrong again, and today he's a respected figure in Glasgow.

To keep at it when you feel like giving up. To believe in something bigger than yourself. Never to forget others are depending on you, and never to let them or yourself down. That was the meter man's legacy to the boys whose feet he set on the right road.

O LORD our Lord, how excellent is thy name in all the earth !

P AUSE a minute — you will find
You have the time to help mankind ;
A cheerful word, a friendly smile
Makes their life, and yours, worthwhile.

THE new teacher had been telling her class about the disciples and apostles.

At the end of the lesson, she decided to find out just how much her five-year-olds had learned.

" Now," she asked, " can anyone tell me who Matthew was?" No one volunteered. " Well," she went on encouragingly, " does anyone know anything about Mark?" Once again she was met by silence. " All right," she said, " but surely someone knows who Peter was?"

At last, one small hand went up, hesitantly. " Yes, Brian?" she asked with a smile.

" Please, Miss," came the reply, " I'm not sure— but I think he was a rabbit !"

YOUNG people these days have a job setting up house and Tom and Isla to my knowledge had a harder struggle than most. They were proud of the one room and kitchen they had managed to buy. Isla was very pleased with a mirror she had bought, for it reflected the warmth and the colour of the room.

Imagine their dismay when one day the mirror slipped from the wall and broke into fragments. Isla, however, was the kind of person who is not easily discouraged and together they gathered up the glass and pieced it together again with multi-coloured stones.

Now, instead of a plain mirror they had a mosaic that added warmth and colour to the room. How often it may be true that when we piece the fragments of life with courage begotten of the splintered stones of disappointment and adversity, the result may be better than we ever imagined.

THURSDAY—MAY 10.

MRS McDOUGALL has had her little sweet shop for nearly fifty years.

And I think the only thing that has changed about it is Mrs McDougall herself. When she opened it, a young widow of 30, her hair was black, and her back was straight. Now she's grey and bent, but her smile is warm as ever, especially for the children.

She was telling a friend about one wee lad of four who came in and asked her how much a penny-worth of sweets cost. Mrs McDougall, charmed by his shy and disarming smile, picked up at least 10p worth, popped them in a bag, and handed them to him. " And here's your penny back, too, son," she added.

Her customer turned to go. But at the door he paused. Again came the radiant smile.

" I think," he said, " I'll have another penny-worth, please!"

FRIDAY—MAY 11.

THE notable preacher Dr. William L. Watkinson was once staying at Menton, in France. He was out walking one day when he noticed a beautiful fragrance filling the air. He looked everywhere for the source, expecting to find gorgeous flowers, but could see no blooms to account for it. At last he asked a gardener, who told him, " The fragrance is not from anything you see. It springs from what you can't see—the undergrowth."

So often it is not the big gaudy flowers but the modest flowers in their shadow that shed the finest perfume in the garden. Isn't it the same with people? The quiet, retiring person at the back of the crowd may have much more to give than his brasher neighbours.

REWARDING

Down on the farm are sheep to be tended,
  Crops to be gathered and gates to be mended,
Cows to be milked and a fence to renew —
  Hardly a moment with nothing to do;
Yet farmers agree, in the thick of the action,
  A job that's worthwhile brings its own satisfaction.

DAVID HOPE

SATURDAY—MAY 12.

I LIKE this little story told me by Mrs Adamson of Ardrossan.

One day, when her daughter was only nine, she asked a question that most of us would be hard put to answer. " Mummy," she said, " what's a good life, and how do you get it?"

Well, somehow, with that wisdom which is a mother's great gift, Mrs Adamson knew exactly what to say. She put her arm round her daughter's shoulders. " When you're young, dear," she said, " life is like a garden with nothing in it—just bare, empty flower-beds. But with every kind deed, every loving thought, you plant another flower in your garden—and the more you plant, the brighter and lovelier your garden becomes."

Too simple by half? I dare say the cynics might say so. But I'm naive enough to believe it—and humble enough, I hope, to keep an eye open for the odd weed, too . . .

SUNDAY—MAY 13.

O LORD my God, in thee do I put my trust.

MONDAY—MAY 14.

IT probably wouldn't happen today, but many years ago the owner of a two-year-old dress suit found it had become rather too tight for him in places, so he took it to the little shop round the corner and asked for it to be let out. The next day he went to inquire about it.

" I have been most successful," beamed the proprietor, " I have let it out to a gentleman tonight for half a crown, and to another one tomorrow for three and sixpence."

THE FRIENDSHIP BOOK

A MAN and his wife were constantly quarrelling. Often it was about the radio—she would be wanting music, while he wanted the news. Then one day he realised how selfish he was being and he decided to change his ways. That evening he walked to the radio and turned on the music. His wife looked at him in some surprise and said, " But it's time for the news." "Yes," he replied, " I know. But I thought you would enjoy the music."

She could hardly believe her ears, and her response was to rise and turn on the news ! From that moment they solved their problem by thinking of the other first.

WEDNESDAY—MAY 16.

WORRY saddens many a home,
  Shortens many a life,
Worry keeps a husband glum,
  Makes an edgy wife.
Worry never calmed a fear,
  Never rights a wrong,
Worry is the worst thing quite
  That ever came along !

THURSDAY—MAY 17.

" THERE are three difficult things," said an old philosopher, Chilon, in his *Diogenes Laertius* : " To guard a secret, to bear an injury and to employ one's spare time."

Things have not changed in the twentieth century. To be loyal, to be forgiving, and to use leisure hours wisely are as hard today as ever. Yet the men and women who overcome these difficulties grow in the struggle.

SERENITY

By sunlit meadows sheltered from the breeze
  Peace and contentment dwell—the perfect place
To build a little church among the trees,
  And lead our hearts through beauty into grace.

DAVID HOPE

THE FRIENDSHIP BOOK

JUDY, aged five, had lost her library book.

Search as she might, she just couldn't find it anywhere, and eventually she took the problem to her grandma. " Well," said Grandma, " have you tried a little prayer?" It seems Judy hadn't, so off she went to her room, and got down to business.

Five minutes later she was back. " Have you asked God to help you?" smiled Grandma.

Judy nodded. " Yes," she said firmly, " and I've told Him He's only got until the nineteenth !"

SATURDAY—MAY 19.

IT'S easy to feel sorry for yourself.

But I'd like to tell you of a brilliant musician who lost the power of his right hand.

He felt he could never touch the keys of an organ again. And he confessed as much to his friend, Dr William Harris, at that time organist in St George's Chapel, Windsor Castle. Dr Harris murmured a few words of sympathy, and asked him to come along to a service which the Queen was to attend.

If anything, that made things worse for the man with the crippled hand. He was sitting there in misery, when Dr Harris came down from the organ loft and asked if he'd enjoyed the last piece.

" Don't speak about it," said his friend. " I'll never be able to play like that again."

Dr Harris laid an arm on his friend's shoulder and said softly, " I played the whole thing with my right hand in my pocket !" Yes, and he had played it before the Queen.

That's how a man with a crippled hand comes to be one of today's most accomplished organists. The musician who thought he would never play again, weaves sweeter music than ever.

F

THE FRIENDSHIP BOOK

SUNDAY—MAY 20.

I WILL not leave you comfortless: I will come to you.

MONDAY—MAY 21.

JIMMY was nine, and his greatest pal was the old collie dog his parents got as a puppy when they were married. Boy and dog were inseparable, and he and Jimmy rambled for miles together. Then came the accident. The car didn't stop. Jimmy found Patch on the road, alive but badly hurt. The vet, as gently as he could, told Jimmy the kindest thing he could do was help the old dog to sleep peacefully away. White-faced and fighting back tears, Jimmy nodded. He vowed then he'd never have another dog.

That might have been the end of the story. But in the afternoon the vet's car drew up at Jimmy's gate again. The vet came to the door with a wee bundle of fur and put it into Jimmy's arms, telling him it was a puppy nobody wanted. " Maybe you'll look after him for me," said the vet, man to man. " I know you're good with dogs. Just for a week or so . . ."

Well, Jimmy *did* look after the puppy — so well, that the vet, when he called back a fortnight later, told him he could keep it if he liked. Jimmy's heart swelled with joy and he could hardly speak.

Bless the man who not only understands sick animals, but a boy's grief, too.

TUESDAY—MAY 22.

A LITTLE thing, perhaps, on meeting
To give a friend a cheery greeting.
A little thing — but who can say ?
Those words may brighten up her day.

THE FRIENDSHIP BOOK

THERE'S a line that I keep remembering at the oddest times: when the Lady of the House puts a brown boiled egg in a blue eggcup in front of me for my tea; when the little girl next door allows me, as a great favour, to hold her guinea-pig; when, at the end of the day I step outside for a moment and take a breath of night air.

The line, by Kipling, is six words long— " Teach me delight in simple things." And this, I think, is the thought behind another verse, by Robert Watson, of Kirkcaldy:

I do not care for wealth or fame, on power I am not bent; give me the simple things in life, and I will be content.

Give to me the birds that sing, or flowers in the wild; a rosebud just about to bloom like nature's new-born child.

Give me the hills where air is clear and the clouds sail nobly by, give me the gold of the morning sun, or the stars in an ink-dark sky.

Give me the trees when they're fresh and green, give me the trout in the stream—these are the simple things, my friend, that make your life a dream.

MRS P. MARTIN of California has never forgotten an illustration of " spiritual growth " given by a woman speaker at a local convention.

She said, " When I was a little girl, I was very close to my father. Many mornings I'd say, ' Father, what are you going to do for me today?' When I grew older, I'd ask, ' What can we do together to-day?' But when I grew to be a young woman, I'd often ask: ' Father, is there something I can do for you today?' "

FRIDAY—MAY 25.

"*IT can't be done,*" *they said,*
  "*And you may as well admit it.*"
So he tackled the thing that couldn't be done—
  And he did it.

SATURDAY—MAY 26.

MRS KNOX, of Gateshead, treasures a faded newspaper cutting.

It tells of the beautiful last will and testament left by Charles Lounsbury, who died in a mental home in Illinois in 1916. Here is what he wrote :

" I give to fathers and mothers, in trust for their children, all good little words of praise and encouragement, all quaint pet names ; and I charge the said parents to use them generously.

" I leave the children the flowers, fields, blossoms and woods, with the right to play among them freely ; the banks, the brooks and the golden sands, the white clouds that float over giant trees ; long days to be merry in, and the night and the moon and the train of the Milky Way to wonder at.

" I leave to the boys the pleasant waters where they may swim, the streams where they may fish, the meadows and the butterflies, the woods and their appurtenances—birds, squirrels, echoes and strange noises ; all the distant places which may be visited, all adventures that may be there found.

" And to those who are no longer children I leave memory, happiness, and the love and gratitude of their children until they fall asleep . . ."

SUNDAY—MAY 27.

HE that cometh to me shall never hunger; and he that believeth on me shall never thirst.

THE FRIENDSHIP BOOK

FEELING discouraged? Doubt if you'll ever make it? You think your dreams are fading? Then read these lines on " the man who sticks " :

The man who sticks has the sense to see
He can make himself what he wants to be;
If he'll get off his coat and pitch right in—
Why, the man who sticks can't help but win!

MRS BRUCE runs a garage, near Ceres, in Fife. One day, when the pumps were closed, a couple from England drew up to ask for petrol. Not wishing to disappoint them, she unlocked the pumps and served them. She took the note they offered, but before she could go inside for change, two local drivers, seeing the pumps unexpectedly open, also asked for petrol.

Only after she had served them did Mrs Bruce notice that the English couple had gone and that one of the notes they had given her was not a £1 note but a £5.

How do I come to know this little story? Because Mrs Bruce went to the trouble and expense of putting an advertisement in the local daily newspaper, asking those customers to come and collect the change due to them.

If you suggest to Mrs Bruce, as I did, that this was very honest of her, she will have none of it. She will tell you that her customers have, almost without exception, treated her fairly, and that she is simply treating them in the same way.

Nothing very remarkable about this story, perhaps. But if the world were full of people with Mrs Bruce's outlook, wouldn't it be a better place to live in ?

WEDNESDAY—MAY 30.

IF you ever find yourself in Sir Michael Street, Greenock, chances are you'll pause to admire the garden at No. 40.

Many people do. Some even knock at the door to tell Mary Borland, who lives there, how beautiful her flowers are. Yet Mary's house is the ground-floor flat of a tenement right against the pavement !

You see, when Mary and her husband, David, moved in, their one regret was they'd no garden. Mary would love to have had a wee corner where she could sit in the sun among the flowers she loves.

But Mary did more than wish and sigh. She declared to herself—if I can't have a garden outside, I'll have one inside ! So she got a green carpet, and green-patterned curtains. She put some pot plants on the window-sill. She grew more from cuttings. She even installed a small tropical tree in the corner. And now I'm told that going into her living-room is just like walking into a colourful garden, for it's filled with geraniums, begonias, fuchsias, ivies and many other plants.

All because Mary didn't waste time longing for the impossible, but set about making the very best of what she had.

THURSDAY—MAY 31.

MY friend John was telling me about his daughter's wedding the other day.

" At least," he smiled, " my wife approves of Jane's choice." Then, not quite seriously, he added, " You know, Francis, a mother may hope her daughter will get a better husband than she did—but she knows her son will never get as good a wife as his father did !"

And, with a chuckle and a wink, he was off !

SEA HAVEN

Around our shores are many friendly places
Nestling in settings lovely and serene,
Where men have dwelt at peace throughout the ages
And city stress and strife have never been.

DAVID HOPE

JUNE

FRIDAY—JUNE 1.

IF, like me, you love roses, you will know the name McGredy. Their nursery at Portadown, in Northern Ireland, is known all over the world. There have been four McGredys in the firm's 100-year history, during which time they have introduced such universal favourites as " Mrs Sam McGredy," " McGredy's Yellow," " McGredy's Sunset," " Elizabeth of Glamis " and dozens of others.

You might think the McGredys haven't much to learn about roses. But that's not what Sam McGredy thinks. Like all great artists, he knows that perfection is always round the corner.

" I have been at it now for over twenty-five years," he tells us in his life-story. " I feel sometimes that I am only just starting. I am still learning and I hope to be a lot better ten years from now."

Surely that's the way in which we should all look to the future.

SATURDAY—JUNE 2.

ONE day in the early years of the last war Tommy Handley, of ITMA fame, was giving a show to a youthful audience in the country. The town was collecting for a " Warship Week," so it was decided to sell Tommy's autographs for 6d each. Among the eager queue of children was one who went quietly over to another member of the cast of ITMA and asked how much Mr Handley would accept for just his initials as he had only 3d.

Tommy Handley overheard what the boy said, immediately gave him his autograph for nothing — and put a shilling of his own into the kitty.

THE FRIENDSHIP BOOK

SUNDAY—JUNE 3.

HIM that cometh to me I will in no wise cast out.

MONDAY—JUNE 4.

EVERY now and again, my friend Jack McKibbin of Dundonald, Belfast, sends me a thought or two. You might find a smile in his latest.

An amazing thing about anybody arrested for disturbing the peace these days is that he found any.

Confidence is that quiet, completely assured feeling you have—just before you fall flat on your face.

TUESDAY—JUNE 5.

AN American businessman who was also a keen music-lover, arrived at a hotel in Chicago exhausted after a long day of business calls. Minutes later he heard somebody in a nearby suite pounding away on the piano.

He stood it for half an hour, and then, in exasperation, called the manager. " That amateur pianist is driving me mad !" he complained. " Get him to stop at once or I will hold you responsible if I have a nervous breakdown."

The manager said quietly, " All I can do is transfer you to a room as far from the suite as possible. You see, the pianist you are hearing is rehearsing for a concert tomorrow night — he's Paderewski."

At once the man's attitude changed. He told the manager not to bother. And he lay and listened with pleasure as the famous pianist lulled him to sleep.

As he said to his friends afterwards, if he had listened properly in the first place he could have saved himself a burst of bad temper !

DANNY KAYE used to spend a lot of time away from home following his vocation as a comedian.

His little daughter Dena found it difficult to understand why her daddy needed to go away from home so often.

And every time Danny returned home he swept his little daughter into his arms and hoped she would, in return, tell him how much she had missed him. But she never said it, and he couldn't understand why.

Then he visited a hospital in New Delhi where a little boy had just come from the operating theatre. Much to Danny Kaye's surprise, the parents did not rush to the boy, but waited patiently until he called to them. When he wanted something they saw to it. They did not smother him with either their love or their fears — but they were obviously pillars of strength, comfort and security.

When Danny reached home, he greeted his daughter with a loving hug and kiss, and let her ask the question and clinch the relationship. And when they had finally got indoors, Dena squeezed her father's hand and said: " I've missed you, Daddy." Danny Kaye had learned a valuable lesson in that New Delhi hospital — watching a mother and father who knew how to give love, not smother it.

THURSDAY—JUNE 7.

A MAN dropped his wig in the street, and a little boy picked it up and handed it back to him.

" Thanks, my boy," said the owner of the wig. " You are the first genuine hair-restorer I have ever seen!"

THE FRIENDSHIP BOOK

AN American psychiatrist named Dr William Sadler once told of an eight-year-old child who seemed incorrigible. Nothing was right for her. She had got the impression that she was unloved and nobody wanted her.

" Nobody loves me," she complained bitterly. And of course soon nobody did!

But then she met Dr Sadler. When he heard her complaint, he at once said to her, " Why, that's not true. *I* love you. I really do like you."

And every time Dr Sadler saw her, he kept on reassuring the girl that people loved her. Soon his therapy paid off. Her mother reported that the girl was now happier at home. Her teacher commented that she was much better at school.

Because someone had convinced her that she was loved, that little girl's entire outlook on life was changed.

I WONDER if you have come across Miss Mint? She's a character in a delightful book by Beverley Nichols. But I suspect she's a very real person, too.

Miss Mint goes through life fearing the worst. She hopes the postman will call, but when he does leave a letter, she hardly dares open it in case it tells her of something she would rather not know. She thinks all her friends share her fears, too. So when she writes to any of them, she puts on the envelope the initials N.W.H. They mean simply: " Nothing wrong here."

I can't help feeling rather sorry for the Miss Mints of this world. If we go through life looking for the worst — well, we usually find it !

SUNDAY—JUNE 10.

BLESSED are they that hear the word of God, and keep it.

MONDAY—JUNE 11.

THE other night I saw once again a film made in 1930 — the famous horror classic " The Bride of Frankenstein." Oddly enough, one of its most powerful scenes is one which stresses the importance of friendship . . . The unhappy monster created by Frankenstein arrives at an isolated cottage where a blind old man is playing his violin. Attracted by the sound of the music, he enters the cottage and the blind man welcomes him as a friend, gives him food and invites him to stay.

He also teaches Frankenstein's pathetic creature to speak a few elementary words. It may be a horror film but I shall never forget how movingly Boris Karloff portrays the gratitude of a lonely soul who has learnt to utter the simple phrases: " Food . . . good!" And, best of all: " You . . . friend."

TUESDAY—JUNE 12.

SIR ISAAC NEWTON was one of the greatest geniuses who ever lived. His work in mathematics, physics and astronomy laid the foundations of much modern science. Yet towards the end of his life he wrote this: " I do not know what I may appear to the world, but to myself I seem to have been only a boy playing on the seashore, and diverting myself now and then in finding a smoother pebble or a prettier shell than ordinary, whilst the great ocean of truth lay all undiscovered before me."

How refreshing to find such humility in such a great man.

WATER MUSIC

The hills compose for our delight
The landscape of our dreams;
Lucky the child who hears from birth
The music of their streams.

DAVID HOPE

THE FRIENDSHIP BOOK

WEDNESDAY—JUNE 13.

W. A. HOOTON was a poet and hymnist, but I remember him best as the man who said, " Try to make the lives of those around you bright and happy—and the trying will be like a mirror reflecting brightness on your own life."

THURSDAY—JUNE 14.

HOW did a jet plane and double yellow lines save a family from tragedy?

A Dundee couple got a letter from their son, a student of 20 with a holiday job in London.

When she read it, his mother burst into tears, for he broke the news he was now married to a girl he'd met only five weeks earlier. Well, he'd caused his parents bother before, but this was the last straw. Furious at the hurt he'd caused his mother, his father wrote an angry reply there and then, telling his son he needn't trouble to bring his wife home. Then he went off to post it.

But two things happened. First, he couldn't get parked near the post office. Second, as he was walking down the road, a jet plane flew overhead. Instinctively, he raised his eyes and saw a poster on a church notice board which said: " Keep Cool — Even The Strongest Steel Loses Its Temper When It's Over-heated."

His frown gave way to a thoughtful look. He studied the letter in his hand. Then he put it in his pocket, and went back to the car. That night, he and his wife wrote another letter, saying they were disappointed not to have been at the wedding, but adding that the next best thing would be to welcome their new daughter-in-law to their home.

They ended it, " Love to both, from Mum and Dad."

FRIDAY—JUNE 15.

I LIKE the epitaph inscribed above the west door of the parish church at Staunton Harold in Leicestershire. The tablet declares :

" *In the year* 1653 *when all things Sacred were throughout the nation either demolished or profaned, Sir Robert Shirley, Baronet, founded this church, whose singular praise it is to have done the best things in the worst times, and hoped for them in the most calamitous.*"

It's not a bad rule of life, is it ?

SATURDAY—JUNE 16.

HAVE you heard of the miracle of Inverewe? There, amongst the wild hills of North-west Scotland lies a large and beautiful garden.

Inverewe is full of exotic trees and shrubs from all over the world and is admired every year by thousands of people. But when Inverewe became the property of a man called Osgood MacKenzie over 100 years ago, the wonderful garden was just a rocky headland, swept by fierce winds.

Osgood MacKenzie had a dream. He had always longed for a garden. But no garden could bear the Inverewe winds that sometimes blew for days, and the salt sea spray. So he built shelter-belts of the toughest trees he could find.

Then he waited—just waited—for fifteen years. Waited for the trees to grow. And those fifteen years I think, are the greatest wonder of Inverewe. True, MacKenzie laid out his garden and chose plants and shrubs with wonderful imagination, but if he had not had his dream and patience to wait for the things to grow, the other things could not have happened.

Truly, patience can work wonders.

SUNDAY—JUNE 17.

HE that is faithful in that which is least is faithful also in much.

MONDAY—JUNE 18.

VICTOR TRUMPER, a famous Australian cricketer of the early 1900's, was just going in to bat against a New Zealand eleven at Christchurch when a little boy went up to him and asked him if he would use his bat. The bat was really too small for him, but Trumper didn't hesitate. He took it and went out on to the field. And he scored run after run. When he had reached 90 the shoulder of the youngster's bat broke off. Trumper played on with half a bat. His final score was 293.

What a day that was for his young fan! There wasn't a prouder boy in Australia as Victor Trumper handed him back his broken bat. You can be sure it was to be treasured for ever.

TUESDAY—JUNE 19.

MRS McDONALD is working as a voluntary helper in the local hospital. She lost her husband a few months ago so when I met her recently I asked how she was getting on. She told me she felt fine during the day. " It's so busy I don't have time not to. " But she admitted that she wasn't sleeping well and found the nights very long. " And do you know what I miss most of all?" she said. " Waking up and hearing him snoring. I used to get so annoyed at him. Now I'd give anything in the world to be lying there listening to that noise again."

I know it doesn't sound very romantic. But I'm sure many widows — and widowers — will understand just how she feels.

THE FRIENDSHIP BOOK

IT'S great to lie out in the sun,
Or sit on the grass in the shade,
To watch children play on the beach,
Or walk in a sun-dappled glade.
For some, though, it's all just a wish,
A dream that can never come true—
Don't forget to take sunshine to those
Who cannot share summer with you.

I'M no doctor. Even so, if anyone told me one injection could last a lifetime and not only ease pain, but cure many illnesses and even save lives, well, that I would find hard to believe.

But listen to this story told by Dr Runa McKay, of the Edinburgh Medical Mission hospital in Nazareth. One night, she said, a nurse there was called out to help a baby who was seriously ill. The nurse gave the baby an injection, then went back to bed and thought no more about it.

Over twenty years later the nurse was invited to a nurse's graduation ceremony at Israel's leading hospital. She just couldn't think why.

After the ceremony, two strangers came up to her — one of the new nurses and her mother. Smilingly, the mother said, " This is the baby you came to help more than twenty years ago. I was so grateful I vowed then my baby would one day be a nurse, and devote her life to helping others, just as you helped her." Then, tears in her eyes, she added softly, " Today my vow has been fulfilled."

So, in a sense, that injection given all these years ago is just beginning to work — and no one will ever know the blessings it may bring.

G

THE FRIENDSHIP BOOK

<u>FRIDAY—JUNE 22.</u>

MRS ELSIE CALVERT of Halifax spent many years working for the National Society for the Prevention of Cruelty to Children. When she was quite young and out collecting, one woman told her she would be better at home mending her father's socks. But she persisted, and when she celebrated her hundredth birthday she asked her friends to send her a small gift for the Society instead of giving her flowers for her birthday.

Mrs Calvert relished the prospect of being able to hand over a pound for every year of her life. Her friends did even better than that. They donated a wonderful total of £264.73 to the charity so close to Mrs Calvert's heart.

<u>SATURDAY—JUNE 23.</u>

IF you'd visited the wardroom of H.M.S. *Swiftsure*, a Royal Navy cruiser, you'd have seen the picture of an elderly man with strong features and piercing eyes.

He served on her predecessor during the war, and not so long ago he paid a visit to her. The crew invited him to stay on board for a meal, and afterwards he sat with the officers talking over old times.

In the small hours the captain suggested that, as the hour was so late, perhaps he'd like to spend the night on board. He was delighted to accept. " Splendid," said the captain. " Just let me know when you wish to retire."

The chin went up. The shoulders went back. The eyes flashed. " Retire?" he snapped. " *I never* retire. I always *advance* !" And the old warrior rose, bowed to his hosts—and advanced to bed !

That's the spirit !

THE FRIENDSHIP BOOK

THERE is joy in the presence of the angels of God over one sinner that repenteth.

HAVE you ever heard of Saint Enoch? You won't find him in any list of canonised saints, but he existed, all right, and I have often spoken to his daughters. His name was Enoch Priestley, an alderman on the council of the City of Bradford, West Yorkshire, in the early years of this century.

Enoch was a staunch Methodist, and such a good-living man that he well deserved the nickname " St Enoch." He lived in the hill-top village of Wibsey, which was almost isolated from Bradford because there was no good road between the two. But Enoch Priestley worked and agitated until a splendid new road was built. You can see it today, proudly displaying the strange name that puzzles experts on Church history—" St Enoch's Road."

There are still quite a few unofficial saints around, thank goodness, and it's nice when we show them a little recognition.

LITTLE songs to make me glad,
Little comforts when I'm sad,
Little chores at last well done,
Little laughs and bits of fun ;
Little ills which happen not,
Little smiles that mean a lot,
Little children at my knee,
Little deeds done tenderly ;
Such a wealth of little things
To my spirit richness brings.

BERRY-TIME

Picking the fruit is fun,
And at the close of day,
As well as good fresh air and sun
They even give us pay !

DAVID HOPE

THE FRIENDSHIP BOOK

MY wife and I were discussing a certain lady, the other day when I happened to ask her, " Would you say she was attractive?"

She thought for a moment, then replied, " Well, she's lovely when she smiles."

How true! Even the most ordinary face can be completely transformed and beautified by the simplest of things—a friendly smile.

THURSDAY—JUNE 28.

SOME of the most useful people in a community are those who devote themselves to one sphere of work — for a lifetime if necessary.

Over a hundred years ago a boy was born in a poor part of Nottingham. He left school at 13 to help his mother carry on the business at the little herbal shop his father had started before his death. The parlour walls were hung with drying herbs, and there were always some simmering in a big iron pot. It was a struggle for them, and he could often be seen with his sister, barefooted, gathering herbs.

Jesse Boot was a plodder, but he built up the business to be the famous chemists of today. His little acorns grew into big oaks with the help of his wife Florence. Florence devoted herself to the welfare of their staff, and if she heard that a poor girl had come to work without breakfast she would order cocoa for her. When a girl married she gave her a Bible.

As a wealthy man, Jesse did not forget his native town of Nottingham, one of his greatest gifts to it being University College.

Jesse and Florence Boot worked for higher and better things—the things that really matter.

THE FRIENDSHIP BOOK

A FRIEND of mine recently appeared as a competitor in a television quiz series. He did very well, and eventually came second in the final, but he tells me that the greatest moment for him was when the phone rang immediately after the first broadcast. A man he had not seen for twenty years had recognised him and somehow got his phone number.

He was on the phone for three-quarters of an hour at long-distance rates. " I don't care about the cost," said the man on the phone, " the telephone and television are my only contacts with life." He broke the news that he was incurably ill, permanently confined to a wheel-chair. A few months later he died.

When I hear complaints about the evils of television I think of its good points, too—the blessing it is to so many sick and house-bound people, and the way it brought two long-lost friends together.

MENTION the name of Robert Louis Stevenson and most people will immediately think of his exciting adventure tales such as " Treasure Island " and " Kidnapped." But he was also a man of faith, and some of his prayers deserve to be better known. This one, for example :

" The day returns and brings us the petty round of irritating concerns and duties. Help us to perform them with laughter and kind faces. Help us to play the man. Let cheerfulness abound with industry. Give us strength to go blithely on our business all this day. Bring us to our resting beds weary and content and undishonoured; and grant us in the end the gift of sleep."

JULY

THE Lord on high is mightier than the noise of many waters, yea, than the mighty waves of the sea.

GRANNY ROBERTSON realised she'd have to give up her house. She just wasn't able to go on living by herself. Then her son-in-law said she could have the big ground-floor room overlooking the back garden, if she would like to come and stay with them.

So she said yes, thank you. But her own little house had been her home all her married life. How she'd miss the friendly door, with big brass numbers and the nameplate below, which her husband had proudly fixed there in 1921. She'd kept them polished all those years, and they shone as brightly as ever.

She went to stay with her sister for a week. When she came back it was to her son-in-law's house. Her son-in-law met her at the station, drove her home, and carried her bags into the hall. And then her eyes filled with tears. For on the door of her room were the brass numbers that had been on her own door. Below them was the brass nameplate, worn thin by years of polishing. Yes, her son-in-law, understanding how much her old home meant to her, had brought them and fixed them there.

So, in a way, you'll still find Granny Robertson at number 17, and every morning you'll find her polishing the nameplate, with the memories of a lifetime crowding back . . .

THE FRIENDSHIP BOOK

TUESDAY—JULY 3.

WHY is it, now that I'm alone,
My dearest memories
Are those which bring the deepest pain,
These thoughts of sunnier days?
And yet, you know, it's just as true,
Though why I cannot tell,
In memories that break my heart
I find such joy as well.

WEDNESDAY—JULY 4.

IN these days of hustle and bustle, when so many noises intrude on our daily lives—TV, transistors, motor cars and the huge juggernaut lorries that race through our beautiful countryside — it is good, now and then, to reflect on the eternal verities of life. These lovely lines tell us how :

Let your mind be quiet, realising the beauty of the world, and all that you have within you and all that your heart desires will surely come to you; and God Himself will come and bend over and catch His own likeness in you.

THURSDAY—JULY 5.

MY wife returned from a shopping expedition in a particularly pleasant mood, not because she had found a bargain, but because of some words she had seen in our pork butcher's. Prominently printed on a card behind the counter she had read, " It's nice to be important—but more important to be nice."

Few of us will ever become important, but every one of us can be nice. It's the easiest thing in the world, and if we are not as nice as we should be, let's start now !

HERE'S a set of riddles worth thinking about from Mrs Mary Lister, of Chilton, Co. Durham.

What enriches the receiver without making poorer the giver ?

What can no one, be he ever so rich, get along without ?

What has no value until it is given away ?

What cannot be begged, borrowed or stolen ?

What costs nothing, but gives much ?

What can take but a moment although the memory of it can last a lifetime ?

The answer to each one, says Mrs Lister, is the same — a smile.

THE sister in charge of the ward where Rachel is a nurse is very strict, even though she is respected for her efficiency. So when Rachel saw that one of her patients was going to hand her a present, she hesitated to accept it, because Sister might not have approved.

However, she decided to take it. You see, the patient was a little girl, who at long last was about to go home. When Rachel opened the tiny parcel, she saw that the gift consisted of two sweets, which were wrapped in a crumpled piece of paper on which was written the following little letter:

Dear Nurse, I think you are one of the nicest nurses I have known in my life. I am going to miss you a lot. You are very pretty, kind, and so nice to everyone. You are never horrible to anyone, and that's what I like about you. Love, Sharon.

P.S. I am going to miss you. I really am.

Only a scrap of paper, but Rachel has locked it away amongst her most treasured possessions.

H

THE FRIENDSHIP BOOK

SUNDAY—JULY 8.

REJOICE with me; for I have found my sheep which was lost.

MONDAY—JULY 9.

THERE'S an old fable which tells how a dying father called his sons round his bed and asked them to take a stick each, then break it. This they did quite easily, though puzzled at the curious nature of his request. Then the father asked them each to take another stick the same size as before. " Now," he said, " place all the sticks together and tie them into a bundle . . . Now, see if you can break that!"

They passed the bundle of sticks round, but even the strongest son failed to break it. Then they understood their father's lesson. By themselves they would easily be broken by the stresses of life, but if they stuck together, in close companionship, they would remain strong and happy . . .

An old fable, but so true of modern society. We've simply got to learn to pull together.

TUESDAY—JULY 10.

EVERY day, when I go home, as I walk along the street,
I see a baby in a pram—he looks so very sweet;
He wears a jaunty little cap that falls across one eye,
I have to lean and straighten it—I couldn't just go by;
And as I fix his little cap and up at me he peeks,
I put my arms around him and kiss his rosy cheeks.
He waves his dimpled hands at me and smiles a tooth-
less smile,
And that's the moment when I feel my day has been
worthwhile.

WEDNESDAY—JULY 11.

A COUPLE were discussing a wedding present, a silver butter dish, and were about to send it off.

" What shall we put on the card?" asked the wife.

" Oh," said her husband — " just the usual good wishes. Anything you like."

A few moments passed, and then she handed him the card. On it was written the words: " For butter — or worse."

THURSDAY—JULY 12.

IN my garden there blooms a magnificent foxglove. Not only is it beautiful to look at, but its leaves contain a remarkable healing substance, which has brought relief to thousands of heart patients. It is called digitalis, from the botanical name of the foxglove, actually Latin for " fingers."

Let me tell you how this wonder drug came to be discovered. The 18th century physician William Withering of Birmingham, unlike so many so-called doctors of his day, was an observant man, always willing to learn. One day in 1785 he visited an old lady in a country cottage. She was suffering from dropsy, all swollen with fluid, especially round the ankles. It was caused by weak heart action, and there was little he could do for her.

On his next visit he was amazed to find that the dropsy was cured. When he heard she had been drinking an infusion of herbs, he analysed the mixture and found that foxglove was the active ingredient.

Two hundred years later his discovery is still one of our most effective remedies. No wonder that when Dr Withering died they carved on his tombstone—a foxglove.

THE FRIENDSHIP BOOK

FRIDAY—JULY 13.

BENJAMIN FRANKLIN, the great American statesman of the 18th century, was a man of many parts and a wide range of achievements, which included scientific experiments. I think the secret of his tremendous output of work can be found in a remark he made in " Poor Richard's Almanac," his first publication as a young man : " Dost thou love life? Then do not squander time, for that is the stuff of which life is made." Waste of any kind is to be deplored, but above all, let us not waste time. With Benjamin Franklin let us fill each day with useful activity.

SATURDAY—JULY 14.

A FARM in the Australian outback had been hard hit by a severe drought. Crops, pastures, dams and water holes were drying up due to the intense heat and lack of rain.

The Jackson family had suffered heavy losses and had barely enough food left in the house. One day Farmer Jackson said to his wife, " Keep the children in the house. I'm going into the barn to pray."

Less than an hour later a man came to the farm-house door. A total stranger, he said, " Perhaps you'll think it peculiar, but as I was passing in my car I had a sudden feeling that you were in trouble, and I had a strange urge to stop and give you this." And he handed over a ten pound note with a promise of further help if they would accept it.

After seventy years Farmer Jackson's son has never forgotten that experience.

SUNDAY—JULY 15.

LET all those that put their trust in thee rejoice.

THE FRIENDSHIP BOOK

MONDAY—JULY 16.

THE other day I read of a Grimsby couple who had just celebrated their golden wedding.

" I had nowt when we got married, and I've got nowt now — but we've always been happy," declared the husband.

It reminded me of what William Makepeace Thackeray once remarked: " To see a young couple loving each other is no wonder; but to see an old couple loving each other is the best sight of all."

TUESDAY—JULY 17.

IT'S sad that folk should suffer pain,
That gallant hearts should break,
That grim misfortune, now and then,
Kind folk should overtake.
It's sad—and yet how good to know
Some friend will understand,
And where there's need, will hurry o'er
To give a helping hand.

WEDNESDAY—JULY 18.

JACK TOPEN, of Inchture in Perthshire, is a skilled modelmaker who can transform planks of wood and sheets of brass into miniature cars and railway engines. When Mark, one of his four children, was small, he desperately wanted a falcon as a pet, but had to make do with a young pigeon which he had saved after it had fallen from the nest.

Mark was very proud of his pigeon, and would go around with it on his shoulder, pretending that it was a falcon. One day he asked, " It's really like a falcon, isn't it? People will think it's a falcon, won't they, Dad?" Then he had a sudden inspiration. " Dad, can you bend its beak for me?"

LIFE should be remembered for the blessings and benefits we leave behind for others.

An organisation in South Shields offered a prize to anyone who could design a boat that was strong and buoyant, and able to change direction in heavy seas.

William Wouldhave, who was born in North Shields in 1751 was determined to design such a boat. He would go to the brewery and test his model boats in a vat. On one occasion he was not satisfied with the result, so took his model to the joiner's shop and cut the boat into quarters. He then returned to the vat and threw a quarter into the water. It floated with the hollow side up, and righted itself when overturned. " I've found the boat that will swim in any sea," he shouted excitedly.

He had designed the first lifeboat. William Wouldhave thought up the idea of building dry docks, too; but his name is virtually unknown. He received nothing for his inventions, and died in poor circumstances.

Those who are rescued at sea thank our brave lifeboatmen, but Willy Wouldhave should be remembered, too. He achieved results that live on — a lifeline for those in distress, " That will swim in any sea."

TO help another on life's way,
To smile and chase a frown away,
To right a fault, reveal the good,
To love my neighbour as I should,
To comfort someone who is sad,
To make a lonely person glad,
To share my joys and blessings, too,
This will I try each day to do.

THE FRIENDSHIP BOOK

THE women's singles of the Wimbledon Centenary in 1977 was a memorable occasion. The winner was Virginia Wade, tumultuously applauded by the spectators at the exciting climax of the contest and as she walked up to receive the trophy from the Queen.

The applause was not so much because a British woman was being recognised as the top female tennis player in the world, nor because she had won the record prize of £13,500. It was because of her courage and persistence. Almost 32, this was her *sixteenth* attempt at the Wimbledon victory. When you find yourself doubting the old adage, " If at first you don't succeed, try, try, try again," then remember Virginia Wade.

SUNDAY—JULY 22.

LET my prayer come before thee : incline thine ear unto my cry.

MONDAY—JULY 23.

THE story is told of an elderly couple who were very set in their ways. On Sunday they invariably went to church. Monday was wash-day, Tuesday was baking day, Wednesday was market day, Thursday was cleaning day, Friday was shopping day, and Saturday night was bath night.

One year they went to the seaside for a holiday, staying from Sunday until Saturday morning in a good hotel with their own private bathroom. " Did you enjoy your holiday?" asked a friend on their return. " Oh, yes," they replied, " and if only we'd stayed until Saturday night we could have had a bath."

FAITHFUL

He obeys his master's whistle
As they reach the rocky tops,
He will guide him through a blizzard
And he'll run until he drops.

He never feels he's cheated
Of rewards his skills deserve.
He works without complaining
For his motto's simply " Serve."

DAVID HOPE

TUESDAY—JULY 24.

IS any sound more thrilling than that of the trumpet?

Douglas Riddette didn't believe that there was. As a Boys' Brigade officer, he taught countless youngsters to play the bugle.

Eventually Douglas and his wife settled in Penryn, Cornwall, far from any B.B. companies. There, on a fine, sunny Sunday morning, he was suddenly struck by what was to be his last illness. He was in great pain—and it was then, as he lay with his family around him, they heard the unmistakeable sound of a Boys' Brigade band !

It seemed unbelievable. There hadn't been a B.B. band in the town for sixteen years. His son opened all the doors and windows so Dad could hear the old familiar music—the last he was ever to hear on this earth. Next day he died.

How had it happened? Unknown to them all, several B.B. companies had camped on a site outside the town, and had come marching in to church, led by their bands, for the Sunday morning service. To Douglas's family, it was something like a miracle, sent to cheer a weary warrior in his last battle, and the memory of it never fails to comfort them.

WEDNESDAY—JULY 25.

THERE are some of us who tend to talk too much. We always feel obliged to join in and say something. But there is a lot to be said for reticence.

Speech is silver, but silence is golden.

Another way of making the same point is the bit of wisdom I once saw inscribed on an ornamental mug: " It's better to remain silent and be thought a fool than to open your mouth and prove it!"

THURSDAY—JULY 26.

MY friend John is managing director of a good-going business, a business built up mainly by John's reputation as a man who would never tell a lie. But once, when a young man, he did tell a lie, and this was how it happened.

He was living in digs in a small town, and when firms gave him orders for goods he would send these up by bus to his main office in the nearby big town. One day he forgot to send in an order—forgot it for several days, in fact. So, to excuse himself, he wrote a letter to his firm saying that he had given the order to his landlady to put on the bus and she had forgotten it.

Unfortunately for John, he forgot to seal his letter. This was too much for the landlady's curiosity and she read it. Of course, she was furious, because John was blaming her for his own mistake. She told John he had better look for other digs. It took a humble apology and a bunch of flowers from John before relations were patched up.

But John often says he has wondered since, who was more at fault—the young man who told a lie that harmed nobody, or the woman who read a private letter. John's wife laughs, and says the real point of the story is—don't leave private letters lying about !

But, of course, as John always adds, two wrongs never yet made a right.

FRIDAY—JULY 27.

JOHN RUSKIN once remarked, " To watch the corn grow and the blossom set; to draw hard breath over the ploughshare and the spade; to read, to think, to love, to pray—these are the things that make men happy."

THE FRIENDSHIP BOOK

HOW long does a good deed last?

A curious question, perhaps, so let me tell you something about the deed I have in mind.

In 1944, Tom Speak, of 97 Sandhall Lane, Halifax, was in the R.A.F., newly posted to Shawlands, in Glasgow. One dreary Sunday evening he and a couple of R.A.F. pals were out for a walk. They had no money, nothing to do and nowhere to go.

A cheery wee Glasgow woman came up to them and introduced herself as Miss Margaret Falconer, 52 Albert Avenue. She offered them tea, a seat by a real fire, even a bath if they'd like one. Tom and his friends accepted. They found Margaret's house a refuge from their service barracks, a reminder of their own homes. It was Margaret's self-imposed task to provide a home-from-home for lads in the services. A place where they could sit by a fire in peace and quiet, to read a book or write a letter.

Not only the lads, but their wives, too. For she kept an open door and a spare bed for any of them who could snatch a few days' visit to their menfolk. Her private war effort, she called it.

Aunt Meg, as they all came to call her, never lost touch with " her boys." She passed on in 1977, but Tom tells me her memory will never fade as long as he and his friends live. They like to think that Aunt Meg appreciated their friendship over the years just as much as all her boys appreciated her.

I AM the light of the world : he that followeth me shall not walk in darkness, but shall have the light of life.

THE FRIENDSHIP BOOK

MONDAY—JULY 30.

I WOULDN'T bother . . .
To explain these words I first have to tell you
the conversation one of my readers overheard in a
Dumfries stationer's shop. Two ladies on holiday
were waiting to be served. One was beside a postcard stand and she turned to her friend, saying,
" What pretty cards, and so reasonable. I'm going
to buy a few, take Francis Gay's advice and send
them to cheer up friends who are alone." Her
companion took her sleeve between finger and
thumb and pulled her away. " I wouldn't bother,"
she said. " Remember, you've the price of the
stamps as well. It's hardly worth it."
A cup of coffee can cost you 18p. A chocolate
biscuit, 5p. If you treat yourself to an ice-cream
cone you'll pay 12p. The same as sending a postcard. A postcard which lets a friend know you're
thinking of her, sharing a little of your holiday
sunshine to brighten her day.
Somehow, I couldn't help feeling saddened when
I was told about the woman who puts such a small
price on friendships.
Then I remembered all who do bother, and the
thousands and thousands of cards postmen deliver
every week. Bless their senders, every one!

TUESDAY—JULY 31.

*I*T'S never wise to advertise
The worries you possess.
Life's more fun if everyone
Decides to grumble less.
Why complain? There's nought to gain
By sounding so depressing.
Let cares go by, and always try
To count each little blessing.

AUGUST

KING ALEXANDER THE GREAT was known for his knowledge and love of horses. On one occasion, seeing a friend having difficulty controlling a frightened horse, he told him, " Turn its head to the sun." The rider did so, and the horse immediately became quiet and calm.

" You see," said Alexander, " it was frightened by its own dancing shadow."

Often we, too, may be frightened by the shadow of our own fears. By turning towards the sun, we can put the shadows behind us.

ABOUT twenty years ago I heard an address given by a venerable old Christian to a big gathering of representatives from a number of Methodist country chapels. He told the story of a headstrong lad who lived with his parents in an isolated cottage. One day he decided to leave home and vowed he would never return. Years went by without any word from him, but each night the boy's mother placed a lighted candle in the window. It was there to guide him, just in case he should change his mind and, like the Prodigal, come home.

The speaker said that the role of our churches and chapels was very similar. In spite of dwindling congregations, we must keep them open wherever financially possible—ready for the time when folk will return to fill the pews again. I often think about this illustration. If we are the faithful " two or three " gathered for worship, we are like that mother patiently providing a guiding light.

THE FRIENDSHIP BOOK

BOB and Jenny, two newlyweds, moved into their first home, an old cottage that, frankly, had seen better days. The garden was untidy and overgrown. The rooms badly needed re-decoration. But Bob and Jenny were so proud and thrilled they at once sent out invitations to their friends to come to a house-warming party.

To their surprise, their first guest turned up wearing his oldest clothes and carrying a spade. He started to dig in the garden. The next brought a wall-scraper and began to strip off some of the old wallpaper. Another guest brought a pot of paint and started to brighten up a shabby door.

Of course, Bob and Jenny soon realised that their friends had been putting their heads together. " It was so nice of them," said Jenny. " We still had our party afterwards and it was the greatest fun."

Aren't they lucky to have such good-hearted friends ?

A FRIEND from Narberth, Pembrokeshire, told me that on his way back from holiday last year with the family, he got lost driving through London.

Tempers became frayed, and as they still had a long journey home, were rather despondent. Then a coachload of Brownies passed, all looking happy and holding pieces of paper on which they'd written, " Please Smile " and " Please Wave."

Within minutes the whole family were waving happily. They noticed, too, many other drivers' glum faces turning to smiles.

It's true, you know—" Laugh and the world laughs with you."

SUNDAY—AUGUST 5.

THE good that I would, I do not; but the evil which I would not, that I do.

MONDAY—AUGUST 6.

I HAVE a pleasant view from my study window, which consists of a single pane of the clearest glass. Yet when I look at the window from the outside, I always see three rather greasy-looking patches. A builder told me they were oil-marks and it was a fault in the manufacture of the glass. From inside the window looks perfect. From outside you can see the flaws.

Isn't this true of ourselves? We look out on the world, sometimes quite incapable of seeing our faults. But people looking at us can see the imperfections of which we are unaware. In the famous words of Robert Burns:

O wad some Power the giftie gie us
To see oursels as ithers see us!

TUESDAY—AUGUST 7.

OLD Malcolm, who'd lived all his days on a croft in the West Highlands, paid his first visit to London, where he spent a week with his grandson, an accountant there.

One day, in town to see the sights, they found themselves waiting to cross Oxford Street. Four lanes of traffic whizzed past at what seemed to be break-neck speed to Malcolm and, after standing by the side of the pavement for an age, he shook his head gloomily.

" Aye," he said darkly, " I'm thinking the only way to get to the other side of that road is to be born there !"

GREEN DAYS

The tranquil English countryside
Charms in a very special way;
Its meadows, woods and hills provide
Wealth for a lifetime — or a day.

DAVID HOPE

I

THE FRIENDSHIP BOOK

THIS is a tribute from Nurse Jo Nunn, of Hilton Ward, Poole Hospital, Middlesbrough, to two jolly ladies, Flo and Marj, who, from eight in the morning till noon every day, make the patients' beds. Every bed is made with care and with a cheery word for its occupant. Jo also tells me that Flo and Marj pooh-pooh the idea that their job is important. But Jo knows otherwise, and she has written this verse for Flo and Marj and all the others who do their service in the background.

You say it's not important, doing what you do. Well, listen to my version, I have news for you. For when a poorly patient is being put to bed, tired and weary, oft in pain, I know a prayer is said. A simple prayer of gratitude to folks like you two there, for spreading clean white linen and pillows plumped with care. How warm and cosy it must feel, to a body weak with pain, to lie down on a comfy bed that you have crisped again. No creases on the bottom sheet, no wrinkles at the head. I know they whisper softly — a blessing on this bed.

ONE of the worst aspects of modern life is that we do so much rushing around. Everything seems to be bustle and noise, with little time for relaxation. Not so for William Henry Davies, the Welsh poet who spent the early part of his life as a tramp and odd-job man, wandering all over the USA and England. His philosophy is summed up in the little poem which begins with these lines:—

What is this life if, full of care,
We have no time to stand and stare . . .

Simple words with a simple message—one we should all heed.

FRIDAY—AUGUST 10.

IF you or I were suddenly asked, " What is friendship?" I wonder what our answer would be.
Charles Lamb, the famous essayist and poet, who
was born 200 years ago, made many friends in the
course of his busy life, and this is what he had to
say about friendship:

" There can be no friendship where there is no
freedom. Friendship will speak freely and act so,
too; and take nothing ill where no ill is meant; it
will readily forgive and forget.

" A true friend advises justly, assists readily,
defends courageously, and continues a friend un-
changeably."

May you and I be such a friend — and be blessed
with many ourselves !

SATURDAY—AUGUST 11.

PRAYERS do not have to be long-winded in order
to be effective—as Jesus reminded the disciples
when he spoke of those who thought they would be
heard for their " much speaking." A short and simple
prayer may be all that is required, providing it is
sincere. I think one of the best examples of this is a
phrase attributed to Bishop Stratford who lived in
the 17th century, but which John Wesley adopted
and popularised : " Lord, let me not live to be
useless ! Amen."

It was surely answered in Wesley's case, and it's
a prayer that any one of us can try.

SUNDAY—AUGUST 12.

A PROPHET is not without honour, but in his
own country, and among his own kin, and in
his own house.

THE FRIENDSHIP BOOK

IS it right to use our churches for anything other than religious services? I found myself asking this question during an Edinburgh Festival when I went to hear a group of talented young musicians perform all six of Bach's Brandenburg Concertos in one of the city's great cathedrals. During the same festival, Bach's Mass in B Minor had been performed—and that, of course, is a religious work. But here was a secular piece written for the entertainment of Christian Ludwig, the Margrave of Brandenburg, and his friends. Was it right to perform it in a church building, with the audience applauding, much as if they were in a concert hall?

My question was answered when I remembered what Bach wrote at the head of all his manuscripts: " Deo Soli Gloria "—" To the glory of God alone." For him there was no distinction between the religious and the secular: each of his compositions was an act of worship.

As we listened to that sublime music, I knew that the large, attentive audience had somehow been transformed into a congregation of worshippers . . . There's no doubt in my mind that we should use our church buildings more often—for any purpose which is to the greater glory of God.

I ENJOYED this little story from a school teacher friend.

She asked her class of eight year olds, " If you asked a person born in 1939 their age, what would be the answer?"

One wee lad raised his hand and inquired, " Is the person a man or a woman, Miss?"

A shrewd question. It could make a difference !

THE TEST

It isn't wool alone she spins,
An ancient pride is there,
A striving for perfection
And a heritage of care.

DAVID HOPE

WEDNESDAY—AUGUST 15.

I ALWAYS think it is a beautiful experience to sit down at a table where a blessing is still asked before meals. The wish to thank God for our food is as old as the human race, and where it is ignored something vital is lost.

Epictetus, the famous philosopher of Roman times, felt this very strongly. He wrote: " Ought we not, when digging and ploughing and eating, to sing this hymn to God — ' Great is God, who has given us implements with which to cultivate the earth; who has given us hands, the power of swallowing and the power of breathing while we sleep.'

" This is what we ought to sing on every occasion. I am a rational creature, and I ought to praise God."

THURSDAY—AUGUST 16.

IN the early days of broadcasting, the most popular story-teller was undoubtedly a man called A. J. Alan. The art with which he told his gripping stories has rarely been equalled, and his secret was that he prepared everything with great thoroughness, even pasting his script on sheets of cardboard so the listeners would not hear the rustle of paper.

One night the studio lights failed while he was in the middle of broadcasting a story. The next time A. J. Alan came to the microphone — and on every subsequent occasion — he produced a candle which he solemnly lit before starting to read. There's all the difference in the world between a worrier who meets trouble half-way, and a man like A. J. Alan who calmly prepared for every eventuality, and whose faultless presentation brought delight to millions of listeners.

FRIDAY—AUGUST 17.

AS I sit in the hot summer sun in our garden, the tiny ants are busy all around me. I keep a sharp look-out for the more adventurous ones, for they can creep up my legs and give me a nasty nip. But in general I have nothing but admiration for them. I love to see them foraging, picking up crumbs or crystals of sugar, and carrying them off to their nest. Ants are so busy, so well organised, such efficient workers, that it is not surprising to find them so highly praised in the Bible. " Go to the ant, thou sluggard. Consider her ways and be wise." (Proverbs 6:6).

What a sad commentary on human nature that this tiny insect can be chosen to set us an example and show us a better way !

SATURDAY—AUGUST 18.

OLD GEORGE is very deaf, and sometimes he completely misunderstands what I say to him. No, I'm not going to relate yet another amusing story about a deaf person. Deafness *can* be funny, I know. But when I'm trying to communicate with George, I try to be patient and keep my face straight. To live in a silent world isn't much fun, and though blind people immediately arouse our sympathy, we tend to forget that deafness is just as severe a handicap, if not so obvious.

So let's try to be more understanding next time we meet people suffering from real deafness. There are quite a lot of them about — two-and-a-half million in Britain, in fact.

SUNDAY—AUGUST 19.

IF ye love me, keep my commandments.

THE PROMISE

The harvest once again is here,
We reap the golden grain,
The fruits of care and skill and hope,
Of frost and sun and rain.

Here's bread to feed a hungry world,
Here's flour so finely milled,
And here, most wonderful of all,
God's covenant fulfilled.

DAVID HOPE

MONDAY—AUGUST 20.

MRS ELAINE BROWN was taking her children to school on the first morning of a new term. Her youngest child asked her to help him find his new classroom—so in she went with him. As she turned to go she heard a voice saying, " Hello— you must be our new teacher."

Recognising the voice of the vice-principal, she spun round to find him extending his hand. Shaking it hesitantly, she said, " No, I'm afraid you're wrong. I'm only a mother."

He paused while her words sank in, then drew himself up to his full height and delivered his reply : " *Only* a mother ! My dear, good woman, don't you realise how important you are? Never call yourself *only* a mother again !"

He gave what looked like a wink before he walked away. But that kindly rebuke made its impact.

TUESDAY—AUGUST 21.

THERE are few stories of Christian self-sacrifice more inspiring than that of Father Damien, who worked amongst the neglected lepers on the Pacific island of Molokai.

One day Father Damien was washing his feet in water so hot it blistered his skin. Yet he felt no pain — the first sign that he had developed leprosy. At the next service in the little church he had built for the leper colony, he preached a sermon in which for the first time he used the words, " We lepers . . ." Never had he felt so close to his people, and never had they been so inspired by him.

Isn't that a clue to the secret of helping people? It is not enough to offer them charity as outsiders. We have to try to identify ourselves with them, and serve them as fellow-sufferers and friends.

THE FRIENDSHIP BOOK

" MY ball is in your garden,"
And " Will you sponsor me ?"
It seems the bell will never stop,
And kids at peace will be.
Sometimes I'm mad—but, oh, I know,
If they weren't there, I'd miss them so!

OF course, we should all be honest, but some people take more trouble about it than others, don't they?

I'm thinking of something that happened to Mr and Mrs Bell, who run the Abbey Cafe in the little Border town of Jedburgh. One summer day, a Dutch family ordered lunch. Then, to the surprise of the Bells they walked out without paying.

Nobody likes to be let down like this. It's as much because of seeing the worst side of human nature as of losing the money. The Bells just had to shrug their shoulders and be glad they didn't have many customers like these.

Then, three weeks later, they saw the Dutch visitors come into their cafe again. They had come to pay their bill. They explained that it was only when they were many miles from Jedburgh that they realised just what they had done.

Though there was nothing they could do about it at the time, the incident kept coming back to them as they holidayed in the North of Scotland. So they decided that the only thing to do before going home was to make a detour by Jedburgh, to square accounts.

There's no motto to this little story — except perhaps that we are sometimes too quick to judge and to think the worst of people.

Friday—August 24.

IF you are ever in the village of Killearn, in Stirlingshire, you can hardly fail to see the substantial memorial to George Buchanan. Buchanan was perhaps the greatest scholar of his day, whose opinions were esteemed all over Europe. He was tutor to King James, the first ruler of the united Scotland and England.

He was a man completely without fear. Shortly before his death, his most famous work, *A History Of Scotland*, was published. Some friends of his went to the printer to see the last sheets passing through the press. They noticed some comments which they knew would be highly unpopular at court, and thought it was their duty to suggest to Buchanan that he might tone them down.

" Tell me," he asked, " Have I spoken the truth ?"

They assured him he had.

" Then," said the old man sternly, " let it remain. I will abide by it, whatever betide."

Fortunate is the nation that has writers to whom the truth means everything !

Saturday—August 25.

AN American pastor once complimented a newspaper reporter on his regular attendance at church.

The reporter told him why he came so faithfully. " Our little boy was sick once," he explained. " We had to take him to the hospital. Our minister met us there and he stayed several hours."

" What did he do?" asked the American pastor. " Pray? Read the Bible? Make small talk?"

" He was *just there*," the reporter replied.

It isn't always necessary to do anything to show sympathy. Just being there can be enough.

SUNDAY—AUGUST 26.

KNOWN unto God are all his works from the beginning of the world.

MONDAY—AUGUST 27.

THE city of Bradford, in Yorkshire, bears on its coat of arms a simple motto which helps to explain why it became the thriving capital of the woollen industry: " Labor Omnia Vincit " — " Work Conquers All Things."

Sheer hard work is the answer to so many of our problems — and always has been. The 18th century French philosopher Voltaire even went so far as to say: " Work is the sovereign remedy for every human ill." In our age of comparative ease and leisure, we should never lose sight of the value of honest toil.

TUESDAY—AUGUST 28.

I ALWAYS like to read of people who have managed to turn stumbling-blocks into stepping-stones, and changed some awkward circumstance into something useful. One of my favourite instances of this concerns William the Conqueror. When he set foot on English soil at Pevensey in 1066, he stumbled and fell full-length. The Norman soldiers at once took this to be a bad omen. Not so King William. He immediately got to his feet, grasping in both hands some of the earth on which he had fallen.

" Look !" he cried, holding up the earth. " This is a sign that God has delivered this land into my hands !"

With this adroit manipulation of what looked like disaster, William rallied his army and went on to win the Battle of Hastings.

Wednesday—August 29.

THE morning Betty's mother collected her after her first time at school, Betty caught her eye guiltily and then dashed back into the school.

" Whatever did you run back for?" asked Mum when she reappeared.

" To say thank you for having me," said the child bashfully.

Thursday—August 30.

THE following notice appeared on a carelessly-typed church service paper:

" Hymn No. 245. Jesus where'er Thy people meet, a collection will be taken."

Friday—August 31.

ANGUS CAMERON had been a sailor and a fisherman all his life. He was never rich, but he was one of the most contented men I ever knew. Sometimes when I was on holiday in North-west Scotland he would take me out with him, and on one of these occasions, a lovely July day, he suddenly turned to me and said:

" You know, I was thinking yesterday what a lucky man I am. There was I in my own boat. The sea was calm, and I had a good catch. When I got home, Bess, the collie, would come running for a pat. My wee grand-daughter would take my cap and put it over her curls. And my wife would have my tea waiting on the table by the time I had walked up from the shore. I don't think there can be a luckier man anywhere !"

Perhaps Angus was even more blessed than he knew. It's indeed a lucky man who *knows* when he is well off.

SEPTEMBER

I HAVE been reading a moving letter from Mrs Alice Hobson, of 9 Springwood Hall Road, Oldham.

Mrs Hobson's daughter Anne was stricken with polio when she was seven. Both arms from shoulders to finger tips were paralysed. Day after day, Mrs Hobson sat by her bed, struggling to coax Anne to keep trying to move her hands, praying she would not face life so handicapped.

One day Anne's nurse said to Mrs Hobson, " We'll just have to trick her."

Anxiously, Mrs Hobson waited to see how it would be done. That afternoon the nurse held out a cup of Anne's favourite orange juice. Then she let it go, at the same time saying, " Quick, Anne, don't let it spill." Anne reacted without thinking. Her arms stretched out and made a grab for the cup. She didn't manage to catch it, of course. But what matter? The nurse's trick had shown all was not lost. Mrs Hobson took her daughter in her arms as they both cried happily.

It was the start of a long process of exercises that finally brought back the full use of both arms. Now Anne is a busy housewife with two healthy children of her own.

Oh yes, our nurses can be cheats. And it's wonderful—bless them for it!

LET your light so shine before men, that they may see your good works, and glorify your Father which is in heaven.

WHILE WATERS FLOW

We delight in the beauty of flower and tree,
  But a world without water so empty would be.
No rivers to sing as to ocean they run,
  No waterfalls throwing their spray to the sun,
And what I'd miss most — no lake lying curled
  In silence, to set me at peace with the world.

DAVID HOPE

THE FRIENDSHIP BOOK

THERE'S something exhilarating about Edinburgh at Festival time.

A walk along Princes Street brings you the world in a nutshell, so to speak, and you can't help wondering at the memories of Edinburgh that will be taken away to all corners of the globe.

It may be the Tattoo, or a favourite concert, perhaps the old castle with its battlements floodlit against the night sky.

Mrs Margaret Coombes, 18 Melrose Way, Chorley, treasures a much simpler moment. She was walking along Restalrig Avenue when her eye was taken by a glorious, deep red flower. " What a beautiful peony," she said aloud, stopping to admire it. Just then, an elderly man in the garden came over to her. They talked for a moment or two, and the gardener learned that though Mrs Coombes admired peonies, she'd never tried one in her own little garden. Before she realised what was happening, the peony had been dug up, popped in a pot and handed to Mrs C. to take home.

Amidst all the marvels of Edinburgh, Mrs C. considers this the highlight of her visit. For somehow, she says, the generosity of the old man sums up Edinburgh's hospitable spirit in a way that she'll never forget.

TUESDAY—SEPTEMBER 4.

I'VE a friend who is a braver man than I am. At coffee the other morning his wife looked over his shoulder at the paper he was reading.

" I suppose that's an account of some bigamist," she remarked, seeing a headline — " One Wife Too Many."

" Not necessarily, dear," he smiled.

K

WEDNESDAY—SEPTEMBER 5.

I HEARD of a man who was trying hard to convince his beloved wife that the expensive new stereo unit they had recently acquired was well worth every penny. He sang its praises, talking about its " beautiful tone " and " sensitive volume control," and adding triumphantly, " I bet you've never noticed that bird song on this record before."

His wife had to admit that he was right. The stereo unit was indeed well worth it to give such beautiful quality sound.

Then the record ended—but the blackbird outside their window continued to sing!

THURSDAY—SEPTEMBER 6.

THE brother of an Armenian girl had been brutally murdered before her very eyes by a band of Turkish soldiers. She had escaped only by climbing over a wall.

She was a nurse in the local hospital, and one day she recognised one of her patients as the very man who had murdered her brother. He was very ill. The slightest neglect, and he would die. And no one would know. His life was in her hands. But as a Christian she decided for Christ's sake to forgive him. She won the fight to restore his health. And when he was convalescent, she revealed who she was.

The Turkish soldier was astonished almost beyond words. " Why didn't you just let me die?"

" I couldn't," replied the Armenian nurse. " I couldn't, because I am a Christian, and my own Master forgave His enemies who crucified Him. I have to do likewise."

" If that is what it means to be a Christian," exclaimed the Turk, " I want to be one, too."

FRIDAY—SEPTEMBER 7.

I DON'T know who wrote these few lines. I think
they come from a longer poem. But to my mind
they say everything that needs to be said about how
we should face each day :

Just to be tender; just to be true;
Just to be glad the whole day through;
Just to be kind and gentle and sweet;
Just to be helpful with willing feet;
Just to be cheery when things go wrong;
Just to drive sadness away with a song;
Just to let love be our daily key—
That is God's will for you and me.

SATURDAY—SEPTEMBER 8.

NO scholar had a greater influence on the early
Christian Church than St Augustine. He was
brought up in North Africa, the son of a mother
who prayed she might be able to keep him at home
to lead him into the Christian faith. Her prayers
seemed unanswered when he set sail for Rome. How
could she keep him from the temptations the city
offered?

But it was in Rome that Augustine, sitting in a
garden, heard a voice say, " Rise and read." He
began to read the gospels, and became a devout
Christian.

Sometimes our prayers may seem to have been unanswered. But often, if we wait, we find they have
been answered after all — though not in the way we
had expected.

SUNDAY—SEPTEMBER 9.

GLORY, honour, and peace, to every man that
worketh good.

THE FRIENDSHIP BOOK

WHEN I passed by Tom French's garden, he was standing beside a bed of autumn gentians. The little blue trumpets, with the green stripe on the outside, were glowing in the autumn sunshine.

" A lovely show," I congratulated him. " You can be proud of them."

He nodded. " It's taken a long time to get them growing like this. These autumn gentians originally came from China. I suppose you knew?"

Well, I didn't know. But I said, " You worked in China once, didn't you, Tom?"

" When I was a young man," he answered. " And out there, Francis, I've seen a whole valley full of these gentians. A field of blue as far as the eye could reach. It must have been a wonderful sight."

" Must have been?" I queried, puzzled. " What do you mean?"

" Well, I never noticed them then," he answered. " Perhaps I was too much wrapped up in my work. But look at me now—proud as Punch over a small bed of them ! That's life, I suppose."

I suppose it is. The lucky ones among us are those who get a second chance to appreciate life's gifts which we once just took for granted.

BE the first to make it up,
  Your differences to end.
What does it matter who's to blame?
  Forgive, forget, be friends.
Mistaken pride is out of place,
  So start again anew.
There must be one to take the lead,
  Could that one not be you?

THE FRIENDSHIP BOOK

A POPE was once walking on the terrace of one of the great churches of Rome. As he walked he was musing on the extent of his vast ecclesiastical empire, its money, its buildings, its network of endless activities, when suddenly his reverie was disturbed by a little brown-coated man in sandals who approached, attempting to speak to him. Annoyed at this interruption, the Pope dismissed him abruptly.

That night the Pope had a terrible dream. He dreamed that the Roman Church was crumbling and the great edifice whose terraces he had walked that afternoon was toppling, its towers and turrets cracking, its walls bulging. Then, just as it was about to collapse, the Pope noticed a brown-clad figure supporting it from beneath—it was the little man he had sent away that afternoon.

Next day the Pope sent out messengers to find the stranger and had him brought before him to hear what the man had to say. So it was that Pope Innocent III met Francis of Assisi.

WE have all met the kind of person who takes the view that there is a catch in everything. I must confess that in my more pessimistic moods I have tended to think like that myself. " Ah, well," we sigh, " there's no rose without a thorn."

But there is ! A splendid rose completely free of thorns. Mine was a mass of deep pink blooms all July, and now it is starting to flower again. And its scent is delightful. It is a French climbing rose called Zephirine Drouhin—and it is living proof that there *are* lovely things in this world without any snags to them at all.

SECURITY

Though busy cities roar with life
We'll keep our secret dream:
A life of quiet country charm,
A village by a stream.

DAVID HOPE

Friday—September 14.

THERE are times when the Lady of the House leaves me baffled.

We had a small anniversary coming up, so at breakfast she asked if there was anything I'd like. I suggested a summer shirt.

" Oh, no," said Mrs G. " That's the sort of thing you should buy yourself."

" All right," I said. " How about a record?"

" Mmmmm," was the reply. " You never seem to suggest what I have in mind for you."

I put down my tea while I considered this piece of feminine logic. " Now, dear," I said, " I think what you're saying is that even if I say what I want, you're going to give me what you think I should want anyway."

And there's male logic for you!

" Oh, Francis," was the reply. " If that's the case you'll just have to like what you get. And if you don't like it you'd better be a good actor!"

Do you wonder we both laughed!

Saturday—September 15.

LIKE so many others, I try to be a good Christian. But how far I seem from my goal, especially when I think of some of the saintly, good-living people I know. That is why I always feel encouraged by the prayer of St Anselm, the great English theologian of the 11th century.

" Grant, O God, that we may know Thee, love Thee and rejoice in Thee—and if in this life we cannot do these things fully, grant that we may at least make some progress in them from day to day. Amen."

As long as we're making progress in the right direction . . . That's what counts !

THE FRIENDSHIP BOOK

ASK, and it shall be given you; seek, and ye shall find; knock, and it shall be opened unto you.

ENTHUSIASM is a great virtue, but it has to be tempered with moderation—and sometimes with modesty. I recall hearing of a young man who was a member of the St John's Ambulance Brigade and very keen to practise first aid. Seeing a crowd at the roadside one day, he realised there had been an accident, so he pushed his way through to the front.

Someone was lying on the ground and bending over him an elderly man who was examining the injuries.

" Let me deal with this," said the St John's man, quickly pushing the older man to one side. " I'm an expert on first aid."

" Are you?" came the reply. " Well, I'm a doctor!"

WHEN the Rev. Fred Smith of New College, London, came to Providence Church at Springhead, near Oldham, in 1862, the blight of the cotton famine had fallen on the village. Most of the members of his congregation were unemployed.

Years later Mr Smith told how, despite their poverty, the villagers gave him a generous welcome. When he moved into the Parsonage he found they had stocked his cupboard with food from their own meagre larders.

His response was to serve them and the Church without stipend until times improved.

THE FRIENDSHIP BOOK

JOHN DUNCAN, of Marchmont, Edinburgh, tells of two wee lads who'd raided an apple tree in their village.

Ronnie looked at their haul once they'd sped off to safety. " They're awful small," he said doubtfully.

Eric nodded. Then Ronnie took a bite, and screwed up his face. " They're sour, too," he said.

Eric grinned. " Lucky they're wee then, isn't it?" he replied.

There's always a bright side!

THIS might strike you as a sad story in a way, but I don't agree.

Pauline and Jim were out walking with their daughter, Alison, in the pram. A small elderly lady came up to them. With a smile, she placed a lovely orange in the little girl's hands, saying to the parents, " This is for your beautiful little girl," then made to walk on.

Touched by the gesture, the young mother started talking to the old woman. As they walked together, she found out she was a Polish immigrant, a widow with her own grandchildren scattered round the world. She never sees them, but that doesn't stop her taking pleasure in other people's youngsters. Every so often, just as any grannie does, she takes great pleasure in giving a small gift to a child just as affectionately as if it were her own grandchild.

As she told me this story, there was a lump in Pauline's throat. And I think I understand why. For above any sadness in the old woman was the triumph of a generous heart.

FRIDAY—SEPTEMBER 21.

IT was especially thrilling that it should be an English girl, Virginia Wade, who won the Ladies' Singles at the Wimbledon Tennis Championships in 1977, Jubilee Year. Behind her win was a background of years of hard work and perseverance second to none. It was her sixteenth attempt and she was a few days short of her thirty-second birthday.

A fitting champion indeed for Wimbledon's Centenary and one who brings to mind a saying that is as old as the hills, but none the less true for all that — " If at first you don't succeed . . . try, try again!"

SATURDAY—SEPTEMBER 22.

IN 1829 a young musician visited Scotland and sailed round the Hebrides. He knew that his sister at home in Germany was very keen to know what the Scottish scenery was like, and on August 7, 1829, he wrote to her, " So that you may realise what an exceptional impression the Hebrides have made on me I send you the enclosed, which came to me during my visit there."

" The enclosed " was the beginning of what is now the renowned Fingal's Cave Overture, and when Felix Mendelssohn reached home and was again asked about the Hebrides, he replied, " That cannot be told in words—only played."

The piece of music he sent his sister—as we would send a postcard—is still one of the most beautiful and inspiring ever written.

SUNDAY—SEPTEMBER 23.

ALL things whatsoever ye would that men should do to you, do ye even so to them.

THE FRIENDSHIP BOOK

A YOUNG lad I know was starting his first job. The night before he was due to begin he asked his mother if she would call him in the morning. Since he had both an alarm clock and a clock radio, she asked if anything was wrong with either of them.

"Oh, no," he said. "They're both working. It's just that you're the only one I can't turn off!"

WHAT, exactly, is faith?

I confess it's difficult to describe it. Imagine you are on the bus from Newcastle to Sunderland, as Mr Hughes of Peterlee was one evening. Overhearing the conversation of the couple in front, you learn that the woman has had a rough time and declares she has no faith in anything. The man tries to point out we all live by faith, whether we know it or not, but when the bus reaches Sunderland, the lady is still adamant.

Just then, Mr Hughes had a flash of inspiration. He approached the woman and, apologising for speaking, offered to prove she was wrong. The woman smiled wearily and asked him to go ahead.

Mr Hughes asked if she'd noticed the bus driver. The woman admitted she hadn't. "Well, then," was the reply, "you boarded the bus with faith in an unseen driver to see you safely to your journey's end!"

For the first time, the woman smiled. Then she said slowly, "I never thought of it in that way. But, yes, I suppose that is faith."

Yes, faith is hard to describe, but I cannot help thinking Mr Hughes' moment of inspiration on the Sunderland bus can help us all to meet the day with a lighter step.

WORK OF MAN

Palaces and bridges, cottages and towers,
Scattered throughout the land,
All were born in a dreamer's head
And raised with man's rough hand.

DAVID HOPE

THE FRIENDSHIP BOOK

A GROUP of fishing companions were gathered at a small inn in the Scottish Highlands for tea. One of them was describing his exploits during the day when his hand caught a cup of tea which had just been placed on the table. The contents of the cup formed an ugly brown stain on the freshly whitewashed wall.

The man looked at the mess aghast, but one of his fellow guests immediately got to his feet and said, " Never mind." Taking a crayon from his pocket he began to sketch around the stain—and before long there on the wall was a magnificent stag with its antlers spread wide.

The artist was Sir Edwin Landseer, renowned painter of animals. And that hastily-executed drawing was the pride and joy of the little inn for many years afterwards.

WILL CROOKS, one-time Labour Mayor of Poplar in London, used to tell the story of a man who was very enthusiastic about the British Empire. He was always talking of what the British Empire stood for and what it could do. One night after a crowded meeting at which he had listened to some stirring speeches, he came home in great fettle, only to find his supper not ready and the baby crying loudly.

Angrily he abused his harassed wife, who bore it for several minutes, then picked up the baby, handed it over to her husband and said, " Here, take hold of your little bit of the British Empire and get on with it !"

Will Crooks added, " There is no such thing as duty unless we take some part of it as *our* duty."

FRIDAY—SEPTEMBER 28.

DON WHYTE was stricken with polio when a boy. He rose above the handicaps inflicted on him by the disease to become a newspaper reporter and a very successful columnist.

Looking back on his life, he wrote in his book, *On The Lonely Shore*, " I am nearly certain that without polio to laugh at me from the sidelines I would have missed something of the essential quality of life. Some men require Everests to climb, or voyages round the Horn. For those less fit there are lesser mountains and seas from whose summits and wild acres the view is every bit as rewarding.

" The more you demand and take out of life the more you have to replace. This is simply the application of a good farming principle. Nothing saddens me more than seeing disabled people without the opportunity and, more important, the determination to join in the great adventure of living."

SATURDAY—SEPTEMBER 29.

A SMALL boy named Joey was playing football. He had been in a missionary school and had been taught to praise God for everything.

During the game Joey ran down the left wing and, eluding the opposing half-back and full-back, cut inside and scored a beautiful goal. His face was shining as he looked up, threw his arms into the air with joy and yelled, " Look, Jesus, what I've done !"

SUNDAY—SEPTEMBER 30.

LET the people praise thee, O God; let all the people praise thee.

OCTOBER

DID you wake up with that Monday morning feeling? If so, you share the experience of millions. It's so easy to be depressed first thing in the morning when you think of what the day — or the week — might bring. But things have a way of turning out much better than we expect. Let some lines of Anne Bronte cheer you up:

Life, believe, is not the dream
So dark, as sages say;
Oft a little morning rain
Foretells a pleasant day.

MRS JOSEPHINE E. BUTLER was a nineteenth century reformer who campaigned tirelessly and successfully against the licensing of State brothels and all legislation which degraded the lot of women. One of the first girls she rescued from the streets was Marion, a teenager from a Liverpool slum. As the girl had nowhere else to go, Josephine Butler took her into her own home as a daughter. Marion suffered from consumption, and, in fact, had only another three months to live. But during that time she surprised her visitors with her knowledge of the New Testament.

One day a well-known clergyman called. He knew nothing of Marion's past, but he went up to see her, thinking he might possibly be able to cheer her up. When he came down again he had to admit that it wasn't *him* that had helped *her* so much as *she* who had helped *him*. She was, he said, " a young saint, so young, yet so enlightened, and so near to God."

THE FRIENDSHIP BOOK

WEDNESDAY—OCTOBER 3.

A LONG stream of traffic was halted at the zebra crossing in Hornchurch. A shopper thought at first that there had been an accident, but as she got nearer she noticed a frightened young sparrow crouching under the lorry at the front of the queue in a spot where no one could reach it.

At last someone guided the lorry driver slowly forward so that he would avoid the little bird. Once the sparrow was safe it opened its tiny wings and flew off. Everyone smiled and breathed again.

The lady who wrote and told me about this says she felt buoyed up for the rest of the day, and she is sure everyone else who witnessed the incident felt the same.

And she comments, " If just one small act of kindness can do that to a group of people, think what the world could be like for everyone !"

THURSDAY—OCTOBER 4.

IT was in the delightful Princes Street Gardens in Edinburgh that I shared a table in an open-air cafe with a young sculptor from Israel. He told me about his travels all over Europe and how he had found the British the most friendly people of all.

Then he waved a hand in the direction of the Castle, which towered above us. " That reminds me of home," he said. " You see, I live in Jerusalem. A beautiful city."

Then he leaned closer and added in confidential tones: " To be honest, I am a little home-sick. The only reason I travel is so I can have the pleasure of going back home!"

I told him how much I agreed with him. Whether we live in some great city, a pretty village or a drab little town—there's no place like home.

THE FRIENDSHIP BOOK

WHEN the *Titanic* struck an iceberg on her maiden voyage in 1912, scores of passengers rushed for the boats in an effort to get to safety. One woman had already entered a boat when she suddenly asked to be allowed to go back to revisit her cabin.

Everyone thought she had gone to retrieve as much as she could of her jewellery, for she was obviously a wealthy woman. You can imagine their surprise when she returned clutching a paper bag containing—oranges.

At that critical hour they were of far greater value than all the pearls of the East.

I AM sure many of us have thought, as winter approaches, how nice it would be to be able to board a plane and fly off to some exotic spot like Tenerife. But I don't think I would care to accept the offer of one travel agent whose advertisement I noticed: " Come and live where you can have summer all the year round " he invited his readers.

Think how much one would miss ! The gold of the first crocus through the snow. The bursting blossoms of forsythia on the bush in the park. The song of the birds on an early spring morning.

Oh, yes, summer is marvellous. But as the prophet said long ago: " There is a time and season for all things," and the good days seem all the better because we have come through the bad ones.

O LORD of hosts, blessed is the man that trusted in thee.

ETERNAL HILLS

Thanks for the strength of the silent hills
On dreamy summer days,
Enfolding trees, and pastures green,
Where sheep may safely graze.

DAVID HOPE

THE FRIENDSHIP BOOK

IT'S always nice to hear about good neighbours.

For Elsie Roden, Longford Place, Manchester, it all began some years ago when her mother took a stroke and was left a permanent invalid. Elsie was just 14, but as the only girl it was decided she should leave school to nurse her mother and keep house for her father and brothers.

Because she was frightened to leave her mother alone for more than a few minutes, she often had to do the shopping in short snatches. One day, while running back from the shops, a neighbour stopped her and offered to sit with her mother one afternoon a week. Elsie and her mother were glad to accept. A close friendship sprang up between the neighbour and Mrs Roden and the happy arrangement was carried on faithfully for 15 years.

It's a remarkable example of the kindliness that so often goes unsung. But something else strikes me about Elsie's letter. It's all about her neighbour, nothing about herself. There are many like Elsie, who give of their devotion day-in day-out for years. Many who never have a moment of doubt where their duty lies. Daughters who stay single to look after their parents. Wives who care for in-laws.

Unsung, perhaps. But not unnoticed. Bless them all.

TUESDAY—OCTOBER 9.

SEVEN-YEAR-OLD Judy was having her supper in the kitchen when Mummy heard a dramatic crash.

" Have you broken that plate?" called Mummy sternly.

" Only a tiny bit of it, Mummy," came the timid answer.

THE FRIENDSHIP BOOK

ABERDEEN folk love to laugh at themselves. I know they're not mean, but they like to pretend they are. That's why an Aberdeen man told me this story . . .

A group of Aberdonians, returning from holiday, piled all their cases on to one porter at Blackpool station.

Overloaded but game, he manfully struggled to their carriage and passed them all in.

"You've done well," said one of the party. "We'd like to give you something to remember." Then turning to the others he called, "Right, lads, three cheers for the porter!"

GOING through a late relative's bits and pieces is not a pleasant job.

Their hopes and fears, their joys and sorrows, laid out on paper make it a sad and poignant task.

That's the way Bill Aitken, of 5 Ulster Drive, Edinburgh, was feeling when he had to clear up an aunt's affairs. Then, on a piece of faded paper, he came across a verse she'd written with an old-fashioned split-nib pen. After reading it, Bill found his job a bit easier. I pass it on because its message can bring comfort to anyone who's feeling a bit down.

It's an easy thing to be happy, it's an easy thing to be gay, when everything goes as you want it and the hours go flying away. It's a harder job to be cheerful, it's harder to do your work right, when everything goes against you, and day seems to turn into night. But cheer up, the worst is soon over, the darkness does pass away; the stormiest night is oft followed by the brightest and sunniest day.

THE FRIENDSHIP BOOK

DAVID ROBERTSON of Burnside, Rutherglen, had been visiting his wife in Glasgow Western Infirmary.

One night, as he made his way to the ward, he recognised a well-dressed man in his fifties who, every night, was there to see his aged mother, in the next bed to David's wife.

The two men greeted each other. Then, at the door of the ward, an odd thing happened. That well-dressed man paused, pulled down the knot of his tie a little, and undid the third button of his shirt.

Noticing David's puzzled glance, he smiled and explained.

When he was a boy, his mother always used to straighten his tie and see his shirt was buttoned properly before he set off for school. " She still looks to see if it's fastened."

Sure enough, as David sat down by his wife's side, he saw the faded eyes of the old lady light up as she welcomed her son. He saw the thin, worn hands lift from the coverlet. And he saw her straighten the crooked tie and fasten the undone button, her face shining with love and tenderness.

A mother's love, and a son's understanding . . . this moving story gives a deeper insight into both.

SATURDAY—OCTOBER 13.

HAPPINESS is something
That doesn't come at will;
It comes in helping other folk
With joy their hearts to fill.
It comes in just the simplest way,
So spread a kindly smile,
For every one that you pass on
Makes your life, too, worthwhile.

Sunday—October 14.

MAN shall not live by bread alone, but by every word that proceedeth out of the mouth of God.

Monday—October 15.

I CAN remember being shown a horse on a farm and being told, " That's Tom—he was with the troops in the trenches during the First World War." Any loud bang used to terrify him. No doubt it reminded him of the blasts and explosions of the battlefield. It was good to know that he would end his days grazing in peaceful fields.

After the Anglo-Boer War a memorial to the horses that had been killed was erected in Port Elizabeth. It is believed to be the only memorial ever put up to horses killed in war. It bears the following quotation, " The greatness of a nation consists not so much in the number of its people or the extent of its territory as the extent and justice of its compassion."

Tuesday—October 16.

YEARS ago I learnt to speak a little of the beautiful Malay language. I have forgotten most of it, but I well remember their unique way of saying good-bye. The person staying behind will say, " Selamat jalan!" (" Peace be on your journey!") The one who is leaving then replies " Selamat tingal!" (" Peace on you who remain!")

Our own " Good-bye!" is simpler, but let us not forget its original meaning " God be with you!" Saying good-bye should never be quick or casual. The warmth of a parting handshake should always convey a genuine expression of concern.

THE FRIENDSHIP BOOK

IT doesn't take much to make a woman happy!

Take Mrs Elsie McGinty of Dougall Avenue, Windsor, Ontario. Things weren't going too well for her. Her glasses had snapped, and though I don't know the cost of replacements in Canada, I can guess it takes a pretty penny. She'd had the plumber in to repair water pipes, at 19 dollars an hour. On top of that, a chimney needed fixed. In fact, as she says herself, it looked a right tale of woe. Then, in the middle of writing her letter, she got a phone call from her son, who lives 2000 miles away in British Columbia, to say he'd be visiting her next month. Suddenly for Mrs McGinty, the sun came out.

That gave me a notion. On my way home last night I popped into a sweet shop and bought a small box of chocolates for which I know the Lady of the House has a secret passion. They were, she told me, a pleasant surprise after a busy afternoon's ironing, and she says she's going to keep me a bit longer in the hope I'll continue to improve!

A phone call from a son, a box of chocolates from a husband. Not much, really. But then, it sometimes doesn't take much, does it?

SIMON, aged four, was having a thoroughly good time in his bedroom, building a massive pile of blankets, sheets, toys and clothing. When his mother asked him what he was doing, he replied that he was playing his favourite game—" mess-up."

Mummy, hoping he might be able to take a hint, told him that *her* favourite game was called " clean-up." Little Simon thought about this for a bit, then said, " O K. I'll play *my* favourite game, and then you can play *yours* !"

FRIDAY—OCTOBER 19.

AS I was watering my pot-plants the other day, it occurred to me that they provide us with a little parable. Any gardener will tell you that the secret of growing plants which flower well is to make sure they are not in pots which are too big for them. It has been shown again and again that poor results come from over-potting.

It is the same with us. A little restriction is often good for the soul. Too much ease and luxury can produce a poor spiritual harvest. So let's try to be content with our lot and not hanker to be " over-potted "!

SATURDAY—OCTOBER 20.

ISN'T life exciting?
Maybe, in the post,
You'll find you've won some money,
Which will take you to the coast!
Perhaps a baby chuckles,
While you are on your way,
You feel it's good to be alive—
It stays with you all day!
Or going around a corner
You meet a long-lost friend—
She says, " You haven't changed a bit!"
Which bucks you up no end!
Life is most exciting—
An ever-open door!
You'll find, if you will push it,
Adventures there galore!

SUNDAY—OCTOBER 21.

FOR what shall it profit a man, if he shall gain the whole world, and lose his own soul?

THE FRIENDSHIP BOOK

WHEN Andrew Watson retired after twenty years as headmaster of a country school, he received many presents and even more compliments, for he had been a much-loved teacher.

But when most of the compliments have faded from his memory, he will still remember the one that was once paid to him by six-year-old Willie Brown, a farmer's son.

Willie had been told that their cow, Meg, was soon to have a calf. One morning he rushed breathlessly up to the headmaster's desk and panted out, " Sir, Meg's calf has arrived. And guess what we're calling it, sir — Andrew Watson, after you !"

Andrew found it hard to keep back a smile. But, looking at the wee lad's beaming face, he knew he would never get a nicer compliment.

THERE are few greater delights than for a father to see his son growing into a fine man. Particularly when the son has physical handicaps to overcome.

John Clerk was one of Scotland's most brilliant lawyers. He limped badly and dressed dowdily, but his keen brain brought him slowly into prominence. His father, Lord Eldin, said, " People seeing John limping beside me on the pavement, used to ask who he was, and they would be told, ' That's the son of Clerk of Eldin.' Now, when they see us together, they ask, ' Who is that old, grey-haired man?' and they are told, ' Oh, he's the father of John Clerk '."

John Clerk once heard a woman refer to him as " John Clerk, the lame lawyer."

" No, madam," he replied swiftly. " The lame man, not the lame lawyer."

HOMEWARD BOUND

The finest day must reach its close at last
  When, tired, we trudge the homeward path once more,
Thinking of all the joy of hours past,
  Another memory for our treasure store.

DAVID HOPE

THE FRIENDSHIP BOOK

MRS YOUNG, of Prestwick, came across a secret when she had the sad task of going through an elderly aunt's belongings. Inside one of her aunt's spectacle cases she found a verse pasted to the inside of the lid, where her aunt could read it every time she put on or took off her glasses. Mrs Young tells me it described her to a T, for she was always doing a kindness to somebody.

Some give thanks for a day that is done, I give thanks for one begun. For the chance to live as I feel I should, and with good grace as I know I could. I'm glad of the chance to do or say a kindly thing in a kindly way, and of bringing, if but for a little while, to the face of another a happy smile.

SOME time ago, I had a letter from Mrs Ritchie, of Bridge of Don, Aberdeen.

Says Mrs Ritchie, " The other day I was standing at my sink, watching the rain pouring down outside the window, peeling the potatoes and vegetables, knowing my family would be coming in soon, cold and hungry. Just then, a thought crossed my mind — we housewives may not always love our job, but I wonder how many appreciate the true value of their kitchen sink?"

Mrs Ritchie tells me it is there that the work of a wife and mother is centred. It's there she prepares meals, fills the kettle, washes up the dishes and the pots and pans. It's where she dreams and plans as she works. It's from the window over the sink that she may see her children coming home from school, and her husband coming in from work.

Yes, in many ways, the sink is the very heart of the home.

FRIDAY—OCTOBER 26.

SUSAN, who's six, arrived home from school the other day with a question.

"Mummy," she said, "if somebody in your class fell off their chair, would *you* laugh?"

"No, I wouldn't," Mummy replied.

"Well," went on Susan, "that happened in our class today, and everyone laughed except me."

Her mother's heart swelled with pride and love. "Bless her," she thought, and aloud she added, "That was nice of you dear. What did *you* do?"

"I cried," announced Susan. "It was me who fell off the chair!"

SATURDAY—OCTOBER 27.

JOHN LOGIE BAIRD ate, slept and dreamt his work on television. Despite permanent poor health, his devotion to research was constant though things were very difficult at the beginning of the Second World War. His family safely in Cornwall, Baird continued to work, at his laboratory in London, on ideas for colour and other developments of his invention.

After particularly heavy bombing of the area, friends persuaded him to stay with them. A few hours later, he suddenly insisted that he had to return to the laboratory and would only say that he had to get a valuable piece of apparatus to safety. His friend told later how John Logie Baird reappeared carrying a small kitten. Its little life was more precious to him than any piece of equipment.

SUNDAY—OCTOBER 28.

BLESSED are the meek, for they shall inherit the earth.

THE FRIENDSHIP BOOK

MONDAY—OCTOBER 29.

I OFTEN wonder just what misunderstandings occur in the minds of the youngest members of our congregations. Like the little boy who was asked how he had enjoyed the Harvest Festival. " Oh," he said, " the plums were lovely. And, do you know, half way through the service two men came round with plates to collect the stones."

TUESDAY—OCTOBER 30.

THE letter in the postman's bag,
*   The caller at the door,*
A meeting with a stranger,
*   What will it have in store?*
Life need never be all that dull,
*   There's promise new each day,*
Just open out your heart
*   To every chance that comes your way.*

WEDNESDAY—OCTOBER 31.

" MANY fears are born of fatigue and loneliness. Beyond a wholesome discipline, be gentle with yourself. You are a child of the Universe, no less than the trees and the stars; you have a right to be here. And whether or not it is clear to you, no doubt the Universe is unfolding as it should.

" Therefore be at peace with God, whatever you conceive Him to be, and whatever your labours and aspirations, in the noisy confusion of life keep peace with your soul. With all its sham, drudgery and broken dreams, it is still a beautiful world. Be careful. Strive to be happy."

These wise and lovely words were found in Old Saint Paul's Church, Baltimore. They are believed to have been written in the 17th century.

NOVEMBER

Thursday—November 1.

MARIE WEBSTER of Gosforth, Newcastle-on-Tyne, sent me these lovely lines:

There's warmth in the house when my friend comes,
It fills every part of my soul,
And loneliness leaves when my friend comes,
And the day is perfect and whole.

There's hope in my heart when my friend comes,
It's there every time that we meet,
I never feel low when my friend comes,
Every moment is precious and sweet.

So here's to next time when my friend comes,
I live for the sound of her voice,
We've so much to say when my friend comes,
I forget all my cares and rejoice!

Friday—November 2.

I'VE a young friend, David, who isn't long married. He's still learning it's hard to get the better of a woman!

Yesterday, he told me he and his wife had somehow got on to the subject of relatives. It was quite a good-humoured argument, I'm pleased to report, and at one point he'd challenged her with a grin to admit she thought more of her own relatives than she did of his.

" That's not always true, David," she had responded quickly. " I've always admitted that you've got a better *mother-in-law* than I have."

" Do you know, Francis," he smiled. " For a moment I thought I had actually won!"

THE FRIENDSHIP BOOK

AMONGST my treasures are one or two very old books. The other day, I was browsing through my 1776 edition of Lord Chesterfield's *Letters To His Son*, when I came across this in his "Rules for Conversation":

"When you are in company, talk often, but never long. In that case, if you do not please, at least you are sure not to tire your hearers . . . Never hold anybody by the button, or the hand, in order to be heard out, for if people are not willing to hear you, you had much better hold your tongue than them."

It's as true now as it was more than two hundred years ago. Some of us really *do* talk too much, don't we?

FORGIVE, and ye shall be forgiven.

THIS pleasant little incident happened to an Edinburgh lady. I am not going to reveal her age but, well, she is no longer young.

One day as she was stepping carefully from the platform of a bus, an assisting hand was placed under her arm until she was safely on the pavement. Her helper, she tells me, was a very nice gentleman whom she thanked with a smile. He raised his hat, walked away, and that, as far as she was concerned, was that.

But he'd only taken a few steps when he stopped, turned, and came back to her. He looked closely at her, and bowed. " I'm so sorry," he said. " I thought I was helping an *old* lady off the bus." And he again raised his hat, smiled, and strode off, leaving a certain lady right on top of the world.

TUESDAY—NOVEMBER 6.

I OFTEN think that for every famous man who is given credit for some important discovery or invention there are several others who had a similar idea but who somehow never found fame. For example, you may well know that the man who introduced vaccination in the year 1796 was Dr Edward Jenner. He had noticed that milkmaids who had had cow-pox were immune from the scourge of smallpox, so he used cow-pox as a preventative.

Yet in an obscure churchyard near Swanage in Dorset I once saw the following epitaph :

" To the Memory of Benjamin Jesty who departed this life April 16th, 1816, aged 79 years. He was an upright, honest Man, particularly noted for having been the first Person (known) that introduced the Cow Pox by inoculation and who from his great strength of mind made the experiment on his Wife and two Sons in 1774."

A gravestone nearby shows that his wife lived to the ripe old age of 84, so his experiment apparently worked. Jenner became famous, Jesty remained unknown . . . another unsung hero.

WEDNESDAY—NOVEMBER 7.

WE have all met people who blunder on, trying to do things in their own way, refusing to listen to advice or the voice of experience. It was for the benefit of such stubborn folk that the manufacturers of certain commodities used to print on the packets the simple warning: " Follow the maker's instructions."

Whether you are dealing with a recipe for a cake or a recipe for happiness, you can't do better than follow the Maker's instructions.

THE FRIENDSHIP BOOK

THE Rev. George Bennett, well known for his involvement in the healing ministry of the Church, was once going through a difficult period himself. The stresses and strains of life were temporarily getting too much for him, so one day he drove to the sea.

He went down some steps to the beach, walked along the sand for a while, and then sat down on a ridge of pebbles which the tide had heaped up. As he sat there his attention was caught by a shell lying on the ground. Its colours were beautiful. He picked it up and turned it slowly in his hand, watching the colours blend into each other, sometimes changing their shade.

There were probably many other beautiful shells around, but this one captivated him. It seemed to have a special message for him, and to hold all the beauty and peace of the universe.

Two hours later Mr Bennett rose, renewed and refreshed. He later commented, " It is important not so much to turn away from a situation that hurts as to turn to something that completely holds our whole attention."

How much we all sometimes need to do just that !

MR A. T. Schofield, a famous surgeon early this century, once remarked that he had been greatly cheered by a message he received when he was laid up with a broken leg.

Amongst a host of get-well greetings he had received a beautiful card from a friend in New Zealand, with this motto : " When you are down in the mouth, think of Jonah—he came out all right !"

M

THE FRIENDSHIP BOOK

ONE of the most moving sights I ever saw was a collection of ear-trumpets. They were in a glass case in an old house in Bonn, and they had once belonged to the man who was born and grew up there — Ludwig van Beethoven. Deafness is bad enough for any of us, but utter disaster for a brilliant musician like young Beethoven. The first ear-trumpet he had was small and simple — enough to help him with his first slight deafness. Then you see them getting bigger and bigger, until the last in the collection is an enormous, ugly contraption, like a watering-can. But it was all in vain. By the time he wrote his Second Symphony, he was almost totally deaf.

So when I am tempted to feel sorry for myself I play a recording of Beethoven's music, especially the Fifth Symphony, whose triumphant opening was used by the BBC as a victory symbol during the Second World War. And as I listen, I thank God that I can hear with my ears what that courageous composer heard only in his mind.

I'LL be wearing my poppy today, and it's something I take very seriously. You see, I had several relations — young men who died before I was born — who were killed on the battlefields of the First World War. I have visited the beautifully kept war-graves in northern France. I have read the moving poetry of Wilfred Owen and Siegfried Sassoon, and through them glimpsed both the horror and the heroism. So with many others I echo the words of Laurence Binyon once again:

At the going down of the sun and in the morning
We will remember them.

THE FRIENDSHIP BOOK

IF Time were something we could buy,
  To hoard or throw away,
Would anybody term as high
  The price we'd have to pay?
If Time were something that could be
  Either bought or sold—
It wouldn't take us long to see
  The fading worth of gold.

Tuesday—November 13.

AN old lady came to see me recently. I won't dis-
close her name or her age, but just tell you that
she lost her husband some months ago and is living
on her own. She asked me to do her a favour. Would
I sign her application for a passport and the photograph which she had to send with it?

Naturally, I was only too glad to help. She was
setting off for Spain with a friend, also a widow,
a remarkable journey for a lady of her age. So I
wrote on the back of the photograph :

" I certify that this is a true likeness of . . ."
Then I signed it.

But as I did so it occurred to me that the little
passport photo by no means did her justice. It
showed only the outward appearance, and nothing
of the courageous spirit which is helping her to
come to terms with her new life as a widow.

Wednesday—November 14.

WHY is it that some folk seem to think that to be a
good Christian you have to look solemn?
" Nice donkey," said a little girl, stroking the soft
head of a donkey leaning over a gate. " You must be a
Christian donkey. You've got such a long face!"

THURSDAY—NOVEMBER 15.

JUST a snatch of conversation I heard the other day between the postman and someone to whom he was handing a parcel. They were discussing a man who had just died.

" Yes, he was always cheerful," the postman was saying. " He wouldn't ever let anything worry him."

That last phrase struck me as a profound bit of philosophy. This man had refused to *allow* anything to worry him! We so often think of worry as something which descends upon us, and we can do nothing about it. But we can. We can resist it, refuse to let it get even a foothold in our minds.

There is no escaping from trouble, of course. It comes to us all. But worry—the great magnifier of trouble—is something we don't have to accept. So cheer up ! A determination not to let things get us down can make life so much brighter.

FRIDAY—NOVEMBER 16.

A FRIEND of mine who once used to do a ventriloquist act was telling me about a travelling show in which he appeared many years ago. In the company was a comic who also did some juggling. One evening—just before he was due to go on the stage—the juggler received a telegram. It brought news of his mother's sudden death.

What should he do? Shocked though he was, he decided to carry on and go through with his act. My friend told me that as he threw the multi-coloured balls in the air he recited to himself, matching the rhythm of the words with his juggling, " The Lord's my shepherd . . ."

The 23rd Psalm has given people strength in all sorts of situations, and it reminds us that the show must go on—in everyday life as well as on the stage.

THE FRIENDSHIP BOOK

SATURDAY—NOVEMBER 17.

VISITORS can be a mixed blessing — always welcome if you are lonely, but sometimes not so welcome if you are busy or pre-occupied. I rather like a proverb I once heard that comes from Portugal, and which one day I *may* have courage to hang up in our entrance hall:

Visits always bring pleasure. If not the coming, the going.

SUNDAY—NOVEMBER 18.

LOVE your enemies, do good to them which hate you.

MONDAY—NOVEMBER 19.

ONE of the most influential gardeners of all time was Reginald Farrer, born in 1880 in the tiny village of Clapham in the Yorkshire Dales. He was a keen horticulturist by the age of seven, and when he grew to manhood he travelled as far as the Himalayas in search of beautiful plants. Many of these — exquisite rhododendrons for example—he established in a little wooded valley near the lower slopes of Ingleborough Mountain. So determined was he to beautify one rock-face that he removed the shot from 12-bore cartridges and replaced it with seed. Then he fired at the rock, and the flowers can be seen growing there to this day.

Reginald Farrer died at the early age of 40, during one of his botanical expeditions. His grave is in Upper Burma, amongst the flowers he loved to share with others. Thanks to his writings, drawings, the plants he introduced, and most of all, his enthusiasm and dedication, he left behind him a fragrant memory.

TRUE PALS

Some folks like a dog or cat,
But you just make my day !
Promise that you'll stay with me,
And never fly away !

DAVID HOPE

TUESDAY—NOVEMBER 20.

BILLY STIRLING lives in Restalrig, Edinburgh.
He's the oldest of four, and one day a letter
dropped through his door. It was from Mrs King, a
pensioner, who lives in a multi-storey nearby.
Here's what she'd written —

I live in a multi-storey, and there's lots of kids
around,
Though sometimes they are noisy, it's quite a happy
sound.
I check them when they're naughty, yet when I pass
I know
I'll always get a smile, and a happy, bright " hello."
There's a little boy named Billy, and to meet him is
a joy,
If I'm struggling with my shopping, well, Billy is
the boy
To take my bag and help me to my tenth-storey flat.
Thanks, Billy — Mrs King.

I don't know Billy. But these simple lines from
the heart of a pensioner show us he's a boy any
mother would be proud of.

WEDNESDAY—NOVEMBER 21.

WHEN did you last talk about your faith? Nobody
likes the sort of person who is constantly
trying to push religion down other people's throats —
but if we really believe something we should not
be afraid of speaking about it when the opportunity
arises. In 1956, when the present Archbishop of
Canterbury was Bishop of Bradford, he paid a visit
to Canada. During one of his addresses there Dr
Coggan took an apt illustration from the local
scenery. " The trouble with some Christians," he
remarked, " is that they are like the St Lawrence
River in winter — frozen at the mouth."

THE FRIENDSHIP BOOK

POLICE Constable Mick Blackwell was engaged in a house-to-house inquiry in Scunthorpe and he came to the home of an elderly woman who was rather deaf. Being in plain clothes, P.C. Blackwell felt he had better produce his warrant card bearing his photograph to assure the lady of his credentials.

The old lady took a long, hard look at his warrant card, then shook her head firmly, saying, " No, I have never seen him "—and shut the door !

A MINISTER was telling me about a difficult decision he had been faced with as a young man, just before he left his first church. George had come to see him to ask for a reference. He had applied for a job as landlord of a public house. The only difficulty was that George was a notorious drunkard, and the minister had got to know him mainly through helping him to stagger on to the bus after his nights out.

" I told George I would think about it, and pray about it," he said. " And when he called round the next day I had the reference ready for him. It wasn't a glowing testimonial. It simply said that though George was familiar with the drink trade, he would need lots of guidance and self-discipline."

A few years later the minister returned to the district. He was curious to know what had become of George and made inquiries. To his delight he discovered that George was firmly established as a well-respected publican. Since receiving that reference, he had never touched a drop of alcoholic drink.

" And to think," concluded the minister, " that I nearly wrote him off as hopeless. What a difference a bit of encouragement can make!"

SATURDAY—NOVEMBER 24.

ALLAN BURNS has lived in Canada for over 30 years, and he wrote to me from his home in Ontario.

When he and his wife were on holiday in Florida, they visited a restaurant called the Hungry Bear. They read this message on the back of the bill and Allan copied it down and sent it to me:

" On this day — take pleasure in the beauty and wonder of the earth. Speak your love. Speak it again. Apologise if you were wrong. Try to understand. Gladden the heart of a child.

" Mend a quarrel. Search out a forgotten friend. Dismiss suspicion, and replace it with trust.

" Keep a promise. Find the time. Forgo a grudge. Forgive an enemy. Examine your demands on others. Think first of someone else. Appreciate, be kind, be gentle. Laugh a little more. Deserve confidence. Express your gratitude. Worship God."

I don't know if there's such a thing as a recipe for a happy life. If there is, surely these words from the back of a restaurant bill come pretty close to it.

SUNDAY—NOVEMBER 25.

GIVE us this day our daily bread.

MONDAY—NOVEMBER 26.

LADY BOMANJI of Harrogate belongs to the Parsee religion, but her charity and charm strike a chord in every Christian heart. Referring to the problems of growing old, she once related how she had gone into a chemist's shop and asked, " What have you got for grey hair?"

The chemist promptly replied, " Madam, nothing but the greatest respect."

TUESDAY—NOVEMBER 27.

AN elderly Dalesman met a young man setting off for a walk and asked him where he was going. On hearing that he was heading for a distant hill, he said, " Well, you won't meet many folk up there. Most of 'em seem to keep to t' lower roads and levels, in t' towns or on t' busy roads." He thought for a moment, then, " Them that doesn't climb a bit misses a lot."

The old man was thinking of the view, no doubt, and perhaps the feeling of freedom you get in high and lonely places. Then there's the satisfaction of achievement, of having exerted every muscle and not given in.

It's the same with life, isn't it? It's easy to play it safe and stick to the lower roads and levels, but, as the old Dalesman said, " Them that doesn't climb a bit misses a lot."

It reminds me of one of Tennyson's noblest lines when he puts into the mouth of Ulysses the resolve, " To strive, to seek, to find, and not to yield."

WEDNESDAY—NOVEMBER 28.

RUDYARD KIPLING, the popular author famous for his stories of India such as *Kim* and the *Jungle Books*, once described how he had been inspired by a text which he kept up in his study. It had originally been placed there by his father, who had chosen it from St John's Gospel. It read: " The night cometh in which no man can work."

This reminder that a time would come when he would no longer be able to write, spurred Kipling on to greater endeavour, giving him a sense of urgency and dedication. I sometimes think that when he was awarded the Nobel Prize for literature in 1907, that text had a lot to do with it.

THE FRIENDSHIP BOOK

PRAYER works miracles. Here is one I treasure :
    Give me clean hands, clean words and clean thoughts.

Help me to stand for the hard right against the easy wrong.

Save me from habits that harm.

Teach me to work as hard and play as fair, in Thy sight alone, as if all the world saw.

Forgive me when I am unkind ; and help me to forgive those who are unkind to me.

Keep me ready to help others at some cost to myself.

Send me chances to do a little good work every day, and so grow more like Christ.

Amen.

IT is a great work to encourage friendships, to link one individual with another. But what about encouraging friendships between whole communities?

The idea of town-twinning is credited to Bill Baxter, the enterprising publicity manager for the spa town of Harrogate in Yorkshire. It was largely through his efforts that in 1953 Harrogate was " twinned " with the French town of Luchon, a spa in the Pyrenees which was seeking a partner. The Harrogate-Luchon bond was the very first town-twinning in Britain, and since that time countless friendships have been formed between British communities and their counterparts. In almost every European country through letters, radio communications and all kinds of visits and exchanges, people living thousands of miles apart have been brought together in friendship and understanding.

DECEMBER

SATURDAY—DECEMBER 1.

THINGS have changed a good deal since I was an enthusiastic member of the Boy Scouts, and the old rules and tests of this remarkable youth movement — founded by Lord Baden-Powell in 1908 — have been brought up to date.

Yet countless boys who have now grown to manhood will never forget the old Scout Law. Especially number eight, which went like this:

" A Scout smiles and whistles under all difficulties."

It takes some doing, but it's a grand thing to aim at — and you don't have to be a Scout to try!

SUNDAY—DECEMBER 2.

FOLLOW me, and I will make you fishers of men.

MONDAY—DECEMBER 3.

HAVE you heard the story of the girl who is said to have been the model for the famous Statue of Liberty? It was December 1851, and the darkened streets of Paris echoed to shouts and were blocked by barricades as young Frederic Auguste Bartholdi was making his way home. Louis Bonaparte's troops had taken over the city.

Suddenly a girl holding a flaming torch aloft leapt a barricade crying, " Forward !" Bonaparte's soldiers shot her dead, but ever afterwards the unknown girl became the spirit of liberty to Bartholdi, so that when he became a sculptor and was asked to design the Statue of Liberty she was commemorated for ever in his work.

THE FRIENDSHIP BOOK

FOR some little service I had been able to do for a Day Centre for the Mentally Handicapped, I was invited to their annual party. To be quite honest, I thought at first of telling a white lie and declining. Why? Because I thought such a party would be too sad for words.

But do you know, it was the merriest party I have ever been at! After tea, we played games, " Musical Arms," " The Grand Old Duke of York," and " Pass The Parcel." We danced and sang and you should have seen the faces of the men in the band as they " led " that singing. I'm sure the trumpeter never heard a note from his trumpet.

Whenever a dance or game was announced, everybody was up in a flash and you would hardly believe how one young woman with a calliper was able to waltz her way round the floor.

It was all over quite soon because the singers and dancers had put so much into enjoying themselves that they were really exhausted. But they had had a night they would remember till next year's party.

Of course, when I stopped to think, I saw the sad side of things. But I saw even more clearly the compensation for this, the marvellous capacity of these people to enjoy simple pleasures. It's a gift that eludes too many of us nowadays.

IN a Victorian household, a small boy was discovered by his mother playing soldiers in the nursery on a Sunday afternoon. She was shocked, and asked, " Whatever do you mean, playing soldiers on a Sunday?"

" It's all right," her small son replied, " they're the Salvation Army !"

THE FRIENDSHIP BOOK

MY friend John was very tense as he sat waiting to be examined by the hospital consultant. He had been round to various departments and had all kinds of tests. What would the verdict be? Was his condition serious — or would he be able to go back to work and lead a normal life?

His name was called. With a horrible sinking feeling he walked into the consulting room and sat down in front of the white-coated man who seemed to hold his life in a balance. The consultant solemnly examined the results of the tests, asked John a few questions, made a brief examination.

" You've made excellent progress," he announced. " I don't want to see you for another six months." John told me that he walked out of the hospital a different person. How good it seemed just to be able to enjoy the simple things of life! And how true it is that health is one of our most treasured possessions.

A CIRCUS lion-tamer was being interviewed on television. We had just watched him at work in a cage full of the most ferocious lions and lionesses. He was an elderly man who looked as tough and fearless as an old warrior.

" Aren't you afraid of *anything*?" asked the interviewer.

" Yes," replied the lion-tamer. " It may sound silly, but I'm terrified of mice and spiders."

To think that a man with the courage of a Daniel should be afraid of such tiny inoffensive creatures! His confession put new heart into me. We all have our secret fears, and sometimes they seem so silly and irrational. But there's no need for us to be ashamed of them, if even lion-tamers can be frightened!

THE FRIENDSHIP BOOK

LEWIS E. WATERMAN was a promising young insurance agent. One day in 1884 he had handed his quill pen to a client who was about to sign a valuable contract. Somehow the ink-pot was knocked over and the ink spilled onto the document, ruining it. While Waterman was absent, fetching a new contract, a rival agent came along and made his own insurance deal with the customer.

The frustration felt by young Waterman made him think hard. Why not design a pen which carried its own supply of ink, so that there was no risk of it being spilt? The result was the world's first "fountain-pen", the name Waterman gave to his invention.

It's no use crying over spilt milk — or spilt ink! Like Waterman, we should use our frustrations and set-backs as spurs to new endeavour.

THE righteous shall be glad in the Lord, and shall trust in him.

THE Rev. Dr Thomas Binney, a Congregationalist minister at Newport, Isle of Wight, was sitting in his study one evening looking out to sea. He noticed that even before the last light of the setting sun had faded from the sky, the stars were twinkling. It suddenly struck him that the sky is never free from light. Though clouds may obscure it, the light is always there, always shining.

Thomas Binney immediately put his idea down in writing and provided his congregation with a new hymn, the ever-popular *Eternal Light*.

TUESDAY—DECEMBER 11.

SOMETIMES one can find a way of overcoming troubles in the most unexpected manner and in the most unlikely places.

A friend of ours was going through a difficult time. After months of long hours at his desk, he decided to get away from it all on a fishing week-end in Inverness-shire.

One evening he was fishing where a river entered a lovely loch. Suddenly the peace was shattered by a loud squalling. He raised his binoculars and to his surprise and delight, focused on an osprey. Something in the water had taken the rare bird's attention. But each time it swooped, it was mobbed by a flock of seagulls. No matter how the osprey twisted and turned, the gulls followed it.

Then the osprey changed its tactics. Slowly it rose in ever-rising spirals. As it gathered height, one by one the squalling seagulls gave up the chase and drifted back down to the lochside. Finally, the osprey, by now a mere speck in the high, clear air, soared majestically on its own.

As my friend laid aside the binoculars, he felt something more than the peace of the evening wash over him.

He went back to his desk a new man. Now he had a new attitude. He was determined that, like the osprey, he would not give in·to his worries, but rise above them. And that's exactly what he did.

WEDNESDAY—DECEMBER 12.

EIGHT-YEAR-OLD Simon went into hospital for an operation for tonsillitis. After the operation his parents went to see him and found him looking quite crestfallen. " I fell asleep," he complained, " and missed it !"

INSPIRATION

Within the ancient city walls
Our great cathedrals rise,
Towering over time and change
To point us to the skies.

DAVID HOPE

N

THE FRIENDSHIP BOOK

THIS is the story of the surgeon and the scrubbing brush.

He's a busy, successful man and his family want for nothing, but when his daughter became engaged, he handed her a parcel containing only an old-fashioned scrubbing brush. Puzzled and laughing, she asked, "Daddy, is *this* my engagement present?" Gently her father explained.

He had always wanted to be a doctor and surgeon. As a clever young man, a university place was assured. But his father was dead, so it would mean real sacrifice on his mother's part. He'd offered to take a job instead.

His mother wouldn't hear of it, saying they'd manage somehow, and they did, though it meant she was up at five every morning and out scrubbing stairs. He pointed out to his daughter that his good life and hers all stemmed from his mother's love. The humble scrubbing brush was, in a way, the symbol of his success and her love. He wanted his daughter to know and appreciate how it had all been made possible. By a woman, often weary, who, instead of seeing just steps before her, saw a stairway to her son's dreams.

I'm pleased to tell you that, when the girl showed her engagement presents, there on the table, proudly marked " From Daddy," was the scrubbing brush.

WHEN visiting a friend who's ill,
And good-byes you have said;
Look round the ward before you go —
You're sure to see a bed
Where you can pass a word of cheer
To someone who has no friend near.

THE FRIENDSHIP BOOK

SATURDAY—DECEMBER 15.

DID you hear about the housewife who, on checking her grocery order, found the 3 lbs. of potatoes she'd paid for actually weighed only $2\frac{1}{2}$ lbs. She phoned the grocer to query it, and her call was taken by the bright youngster who'd started work in the shop that week.

" Ah, yes, ma'am," he said confidently, " I made up your order myself. You see, some of the potatoes were bad, so I took the liberty of throwing them out for you."

A young man who should go far !

SUNDAY—DECEMBER 16.

HEAVEN and earth shall pass away : but my words shall not pass away.

MONDAY—DECEMBER 17.

THIS appeared in a church magazine. I pass it on without comment —

It's just a good thing God above has never gone on strike because he wasn't treated fair on things he didn't like. If he had ever once sat down and said, " That's it, I'm through. I've had enough of those on earth — so this is what I'll do.

I'll give my orders to the sun, cut off your heat supply, and to the moon give no more light, and run the oceans dry. Then just to make it really tough and put the pressure on — turn off the air and oxygen till every breath is gone."

Men say they want a better deal and so on strike they go. But what a deal we've given God, to whom the world we owe ! We don't much care whom we hurt to gain the things we like. But what a mess we'd all be in if God should go on strike !

THE FRIENDSHIP BOOK

HOW can being seriously ill and losing your job change your life for the better?

Mrs B. used to work full time, but for some reason it made her, she admits, a shocker to live with. Time and again she would tell her husband she didn't need him, that she could keep herself. Then she had a serious stroke. Convalescent for weeks that spun out into months, she found herself completely dependent on her husband.

In all that time he never once reminded her of her hard words. Gradually, as she saw him struggle uncomplainingly with the shopping, the housework and the cooking, she realised what a fool she had been.

Now she's well on the road to recovery. And she realises how lucky she is. From being a bitter, resentful woman with a chip on her shoulder, she is going forward with a new attitude to her husband, to her marriage and to life itself. But how she rues the wasted years . . .

That's Mrs B.'s story. I leave you to take your own message from it.

I NOTICED a group of youngsters the other day, laughing uproariously at some clown who was entertaining them. It turned out to be old Harry, who is in his late seventies. There he was sitting in the middle of these lads and lasses, cracking jokes, pulling their legs, and generally having fun.

And I thought of that wise observation of the American doctor and humorist, Oliver Wendell Holmes:

" *To be seventy years young is sometimes far more cheerful and hopeful than to be forty years old.*"

MY WISH

Some folk like a lot of noise,
With crowds all having fun;
But give me peace — and best of all
A corner in the sun.

DAVID HOPE

THE FRIENDSHIP BOOK

THERE was a ring at the door of a house in Glasgow one night.

When the woman who lives there answered it she found a stranger on the step with a message from her 16-year-old daughter. The girl had run away a month earlier. The family hadn't heard from her since and they had been worried sick. The message told them that she was safe and well.

It came through a lifeline service to help runaway Scots youngsters down south, organised by the Mothers' Union, who've opened centres in London, Liverpool and Birmingham. There, runaways can call or phone to leave a message for worried parents.

Youngsters phoning any of the centres are greeted by a recorded message, which invites them to leave their name and home address, and record a message for the family.

The service is strictly confidential. Mothers' Union don't aim to reunite families, though they hope it may often lead to this. But their first aim is simply to set parents' minds at rest. The messages are relayed to the runaways' home towns where a member of the Mothers' Union delivers it personally.

It's so very easy to lose touch. I have a feeling many parents — and youngsters — will have cause to be grateful to the Mothers' Union.

I'M indebted to a young mother for this little conversation she overheard.

Eileen, aged five, asked her six-year-old brother seriously, " Did God really make everything?"

Without hesitation he replied, " Oh, no, Daddy made the kitchen cupboards."

SATURDAY—DECEMBER 22.

THE staff at Dundee's Liff Hospital were told that there could be no money allocated to ward funds because of the country's economic plight. This meant that there would be no Christmas party for the patients.

That could have been the end of this story, but it isn't. For instead of just accepting the situation as they could so easily have done, the nurses set to and organised a sale of work. Within four days they had cooked and baked enough to feed a small army. Five days after the bad news had been broken, they had raised more money than they required.

Well done, everyone!

SUNDAY—DECEMBER 23.

AND she shall bring forth a son, and thou shalt call his name Jesus : for he shall save his people from their sins.

MONDAY—DECEMBER 24.

GEORGE HERBERT, who died in 1632 at the age of 39, was a saintly vicar whose cheerful hymns have become great favourites.

Christians of all denominations sing, for example, " Let All the World in Every Corner Sing," " King of Glory, King of Peace," and " Teach me my God and King."

Less well known is his beautifully simple prayer for gratitude. When I find that I am taking too many good things for granted I sometimes repeat George Herbert's words, " Thou who hast given so much to me, give one thing more—a grateful heart. Amen."

THE FRIENDSHIP BOOK

> " *I'M* very strong," said the tiger,
>   " And I am brave," said the bear.
> " And I must rule," said the lion,
>   Confident in his lair.
> And then, in a little whisper,
>   There came the voice of the ass —
> " I'm nothing much to look at,
>   I'm not in the others' class;
> But no-one can deny it,
>   I've got the better of them —
> For Mary rode upon my back,
>   As we entered Bethlehem !"

I LIKE the story I heard recently as an illustration of the text " By their fruits ye shall know them."

A little boy had had a terrible squabble with his sister, and not long afterwards she complained that her favourite rag doll was missing. The family made a careful search for it all over the house, but it could not be found, and the boy claimed he knew nothing about it.

The following spring the little girl noticed something very odd in the garden. Sprouting from the soil were scores of little green shoots in the shape of a doll. She carefully scraped away the soil from the shoots and found her treasured rag doll underneath. Her brother had buried it — but his secret had been revealed, for the oats with which it was stuffed had sprung to life in the moist darkness of the earth.

A nice illustration of the fact that we are known by our fruits, and that we can be sure our sins will find us out !

EVENING GLORY

At every e'en the clouds and sun
    Enact their ancient, ever-changing story,
And puny man, his daily labours done,
    Watches with awe the many-splendoured glory.

DAVID HOPE

THE FRIENDSHIP BOOK

THERE'S a lot to be learned from the mistake made by a famous English cricketer who was handed a sealed envelope one September during the last match of the season. He was just ready to go out on the field, so he popped the letter in his pocket.

When he got out his cricketing clothes the following April he found the crumpled letter, still in his pocket. When he opened it he was amazed — and shocked — to find that it was an invitation to play for England in Australia during the winter that had just passed.

Strange, isn't it, how some of the great things in life depend on attention to small details? I think I'll make a New Year resolution to open my letters as soon as I receive them — and answer them pretty promptly, as well!

HAVE you ever heard of the Focolare Movement? Its name derives from the Italian word for "fireside," which well sums up the movement's aims to spread Christian love and fellowship. It was started in 1943 by a young Italian woman of 23 called Chiara Lubich. Now there are 217 centres — or "firesides" — in 33 countries, and these include hospitals and social centres.

In 1977 Chiara was awarded the Templeton Foundation Prize for Progress in Religion, which, I am told, is the equivalent of £50,000. When she publicly accepted this money on behalf of the Focolare Movement she concluded her address with some words by the Spanish mystic, St John of the Cross, to sum up her philosophy: "Where you do not find love, put love — and then you *will* find love!"

THE FRIENDSHIP BOOK

SATURDAY—DECEMBER 29.

I RECENTLY went to the re-opening and dedication of a new church. The old building had proved too expensive to maintain and heat, so the congregation had reluctantly decided to turn the Sunday School hall into a dual-purpose building. The architect, one of their own members, had made a first-class job of the conversion and the result was both practical and dignified.

But what impressed me during the re-opening service was not so much the building as the sight of the architect's three fine teenage sons, welcoming folk in the vestibule, showing visitors round, helping to take the collection.

A church, after all, is not a building. It's a group of people — particularly young people, who are the only real foundations on which we can build for the future.

SUNDAY—DECEMBER 30.

THE Lord is good unto them that wait for him, to the soul that seeketh him.

MONDAY—DECEMBER 31.

IT is often assumed that scientific men are likely to be unbelievers, or even anti-religious. This is far from being the case, and some have been devout Christians. Take, for example, Sir James Young Simpson, whose statue can be seen in Princes Street, Edinburgh. He is famous for the introduction of chloroform, and during his lifetime he was highly acclaimed as pioneer of modern surgery. One day he was asked what he considered his greatest discovery. Simpson simply replied, " That I have a Saviour."

Where the Photographs were taken

WINTRY DAYS — *Dundonald Castle, nr. Troon, Ayrshire.*
ROUGH BEAUTY — *Tintagel, Cornwall.*
IN HARBOUR — *Lossiemouth, Moray.*
SINGING RIVER — *Dean Bridge, Edinburgh.*
REAPING THE SEA — *Seaton, Devon.*
HER HERO — *Cardiff Castle, Glamorgan.*
TREASURE TROVE — *Crowmarsh Gifford, Oxfordshire.*
SPRING SONG — *Court of Noke, Staunton-on-Arrow, Herefordshire.*
HARMONY — *Symond's Yat, Hereford/Gloucestershire.*
WELCOME — *The Latchetts, Eardisland, Herefordshire.*
REWARDING — *Troutbeck, Cumberland.*
SERENITY — *Stanway Church, nr. Winchcomb, Gloucestershire.*
SEA HAVEN — *Oban, Argyll.*
WATER MUSIC — *Ashness Bridge, Cumberland.*
FAITHFUL — *Saunderton, Buckinghamshire.*
GREEN DAYS — *Hambleden Lock, Buckinghamshire.*
THE TEST — *Drinesheader, Harris, Outer Hebrides, Inverness-shire.*
THE PROMISE — *Marcle Hill, Herefordshire.*
WHILE WATERS FLOW — *Horseshoe Falls, River Dee, Llangollen.*
SECURITY — *Buckland in the Moor, Devon.*
WORK OF MAN — *Clifton Bridge, Bristol.*
ETERNAL HILLS — *Newlands Valley, Cumberland.*
HOMEWARD BOUND — *Mudeford, Christchurch, Hampshire.*
INSPIRATION — *York.*
MY WISH — *Corrie, Arran, Bute.*
EVENING GLORY — *Bromsgrove, Worcestershire.*

Printed and Published by D. C. THOMSON & CO., LTD.,
185 Fleet Street, London EC4A 2HS.
© D. C. Thomson & Co., Ltd., 1978.